The Heart Is Noble

The Heart
Is Noble

*Changing the World
From the Inside Out*

HIS HOLINESS THE KARMAPA
Ogyen Trinley Dorje

TRANSLATED BY
Ngodup Tsering Burkhar &
Damchö Diana Finnegan, PhD

EDITED BY
Karen Derris, PhD &
Damchö Diana Finnegan, PhD

 SHAMBHALA · *Boston & London* · 2014

Shambhala Publications, Inc.
Horticultural Hall
300 Massachusetts Avenue
Boston, Massachusetts 02115
www.shambhala.com

9 8 7 6 5 4 3 2 1

First Paperback Edition
Printed in the United States of America

♾ This edition is printed on acid-free paper that meets the American National Standards Institute Z39.48 Standard.
♻ This book is printed on 30% postconsumer recycled paper.
For more information please visit www.shambhala.com.

Distributed in the United States by Penguin Random House LLC and in Canada by Random House of Canada Ltd

Designed by Lora Zorian

THE LIBRARY OF CONGRESS CATALOGUES THE HARDCOVER EDITION OF THIS BOOK AS FOLLOWS:

O-rgyan-'phrin-las-rdo-rje, Karma-pa XVII, 1985–
The heart is noble: changing the world from the inside out / His Holiness the Karmapa, Ogyen Trinley Dorje; translated by Ngodup Tsering Burkhar and Damchö Diana Finnegan, PhD; edited by Karen Derris, PhD, and Damchö Diana Finnegan, PhD.
—First edition.
pages   cm
Includes translations from Tibetan.
ISBN 978-1-61180-001-2 (hardcover: alk. paper)
ISBN 978-1-61180-080-7 (paperback: alk. paper)
1. Buddhism and social problems. 2. Buddhism and humanism.
3. Religious life—Kar-ma-pa (Sect). I. Finnegan, Diana, editor, translator.
II. Derris, Karen, editor. III. Title.
BQ7950.O764H43 2013
294.3'376—dc23
2012046101

Contents

    and Joy   160

12. Living the Teachings   175

    Editors' Acknowledgments   185

    A Biography of His Holiness the Karmapa   187

    Editors' and Translators' Biographies   191

THE DALAI LAMA

IT GIVES ME GREAT PLEASURE to introduce this new book by the Seventeenth Karmapa, Ogyen Trinley Dorje, a young man who has been studying well and working hard to fulfill his responsibilities as head of the Kamtsang Kagyu tradition of Tibetan Buddhism.

These days I draw a distinction between people like me in their sixties and seventies who belong to the twentieth century, an era that has passed, and those in their teens, twenties, and thirties; this twenty-first century will be for them to shape. Humanity made remarkable progress in the twentieth century in fields like medicine, travel, and communications, but it was also a period of conflict and bloodshed that we want never to see again. If the coming decades are going to be significantly different, today's young people need to find ways of securing peace in the world based on establishing inner peace within themselves and relying on dialogue to deal with whatever problems arise.

I am encouraged that this book came about as a consequence of the interaction between the Karmapa Rinpoche and a group of young, intelligent American university students. The result is not so much a presentation of a Buddhist point of view, but an example of the contribution Buddhist ideas can make to contemporary conversation. Rinpoche repeatedly explains how we can tap into our basic good human qualities, the noble heart of the title, as a source of good motivation and positive action. The important thing is to go beyond mere good wishes to actually taking action, whether it concerns dealing with emotions and transforming the mind or steps to protect the natural environment.

I am sure that readers who pay attention to what is discussed here and try it out in their own lives will not only feel happier within themselves, but will also contribute to making a happier, more peaceful world for the twenty-first century.

Tenzin Gyatso, the Fourteenth Dalai Lama
October 3, 2012

Editors' Preface

THE SPIRITUAL TEACHER whose words of wisdom are contained in this book is known to many as "His Holiness the Karmapa." In May 2011, His Holiness adjusted his demanding schedule in order to make time for a series of meetings with a group of sixteen American college students at his residence in India. The teachings he gave to them during the course of that month form the basis of this book.

The students had their first glimpse of His Holiness the Karmapa at his semiweekly public audience, held in the assembly hall of Gyuto Monastery in north India. The Karmapa is one of the highest-ranking lamas in Tibetan Buddhism, and a large crowd had gathered. As everyone present lined up and then passed briefly before the Karmapa to receive his blessing, the students found themselves intimidated by his serenity and majestic bearing. This initial encounter with the Karmapa brought home for them just how exceptional it was to have this opportunity to share three weeks of private conversations with him.

Later that day, the students filed into the Karmapa's library for their first private meeting. They peered surreptitiously around the airy, modern library, which was filled with Tibetan texts and books from around the world. As the students were introduced to the Karmapa one by one, they approached him to offer their gifts. Many were handmade especially for him, including paintings, a sculpture, chocolate truffles, and even a banjo. It seemed clear to everyone that the students were offering a bit of themselves, and that His Holiness was receiving the offerings with genuine curiosity and an open heart. When the students returned the following day for their second session, they saw that many of their gifts were displayed on the bookshelves surrounding the sitting area. Although they had arrived unsure of their place in this unfamiliar environment, the students were reassured by this sign that they were a welcome presence in His Holiness's space.

The project had its start a year earlier, when the Karmapa authorized one of his students, an American nun named Damchö, to contact her longtime friend Karen Derris, a professor of religious studies, to discuss bringing a group of college students for an extended visit with him. With the enthusiastic support of the University of Redlands, Karen agreed to lead a class from the school, a liberal arts university in Southern California. (Damchö and Karen then organized the student visit, and later coedited this book.)

In keeping with the Karmapa's wish to take as the starting point what the students wanted to hear from Buddhism, rather than what Buddhism had to say to them, Damchö and Karen sent an informal survey to a large number of Karen's students, asking what they would most like to learn from a Buddhist spiritual leader. The students' responses suggested a hunger for an opportunity to explore their concerns with a teacher who could offer them new perspectives on the world and on their own lives. The topics selected for the sessions—the same topics that now appear as the chapters of this book—grew from the students' suggestions.

Prior to their trip to India in May, the group spent the winter months preparing for their visit with the Karmapa. From their earliest meetings for the trip, Karen cautioned the students against bringing their own expectations to the experience. They set themselves the goal of responding to whatever was presented, since none of them, the professor included, could fully imagine what the experience would be like once they were in India with the

Karmapa. The students committed to being open to whatever was offered or asked of them.

The project also envisioned having the students move beyond a passive role in the encounter, and actively sharing their hopes and concerns with the Karmapa. Among the student group were activists whose work ranged from labor rights to interreligious dialogue to food justice. During the course of their meetings with the Karmapa, the students described for him their dreams of what they might contribute to the world, as well as their personal life experiences. He reflected back to them their sincerity and wish to care for each other and the world, and showed them that they needed nothing else in order to be worthy of this encounter. Anyone with an open heart and good intentions was fully qualified to receive and make full use of his teachings.

The students were clearly humbled by this opportunity, but they were also brave, adventurous, and willing to try out different ways of being in the world. They took pains to be respectful of Tibetan cultural expectations and Buddhist ethical guidelines. In the initial meetings about the course, Karen stipulated that a condition for joining the trip would be their commitment to observe the five Buddhist precepts—refraining from killing, stealing, untruthful speech, sexual misconduct, and intoxicants—during the entirety of their stay in India. The students would be able to learn the significance of the precepts by applying them to the particulars of their experience. Not taking life would include keeping a vegetarian diet, as inspired by the Karmapa's vision of vegetarianism as a central ethical and activist issue; not taking what is not given would be the basis for actively reflecting upon the resources they used while staying in the small village of Sidhpur; avoiding untruthful speech would help them to be mindful of the ways in which they communicated with one another; and not partaking of any kind of intoxicant would help them keep their minds clear and present at all times.

The students all voluntarily fulfilled this commitment to live by the precepts for the month of their stay, and many later reflected that this was an important part of their experience of self-discovery. On an outing they took together to a nearby Tibetan cultural institute, His Holiness teased the students as they sat together for tea, saying that their behavior was so proper that they were acting like monks and nuns.

Inspired by the Karmapa's teachings, his generosity, and the care they received from those around him, the students were motivated to work hard. They often spent twelve hours a day in formal sessions—preparing before teachings, receiving teachings, and then collectively reviewing and processing the ideas and perspectives they had just encountered. Despite their already long days, the students were often inspired to go back over the steps of His Holiness's arguments in order to explore the subtleties of his teachings. This was especially true of the sessions when the Karmapa offered them radically different paradigms for understanding themselves and the world, such as the view that greed is not an innate quality, or that habit is an important basis for relationships.

Yet what was most remarkable was not the amount of time the students spent, but the spirit they brought to their work. As students of the University of Redlands's Johnston Center for Integrative Studies, they adeptly applied the collaborative ethos of Johnston's living-learning community to this cross-cultural experience. They were not only intellectual risk takers; they were also skilled in consensus-based learning. When any student was speaking during a session with the Karmapa, the student consistently voiced ideas that had been developed with the whole group, rather than just speaking for himself or herself as an individual. In this way, the students approached learning not as something to acquire for themselves, but as something to contribute to and share with others.

Throughout their month together, His Holiness the Karmapa extended himself to the students in love and friendship. At one point, a student commented that although they were peers of the Karmapa in terms of age, they were not his peers in any other sense. Witnessing the profound wisdom that His Holiness exhibits already made a deep impression on the students, who were only a few years younger than he was.

However, he is not simply an exceptional teacher for his young age. He is considered by Tibetan Buddhists to have been successively reincarnating as the Karmapa for nine hundred years. As such, from one perspective he was just twenty-five years old at the time of this meeting. From another, he was nine hundred years old, a fact that he himself joked about with the students. In their time with him, the Karmapa seamlessly projected both of these identities as one, allowing his youth to serve as a skillful means to reach the students, even as his ageless wisdom gave him an unapproachable depth to teach from. His humorous references to popular culture, such as iPhones and comic book characters, were moments of connection that bridged the divide of such widely divergent life experiences and spiritual accomplishments.

The necessities of observing forms of respect were always present, but His Holiness consistently acted to ensure that this did not present a barrier to warmth and deep personal connections. Ngodup Tsering Burkhar, His Holiness's translator, skillfully communicated not only the meaning of the Karmapa's words to the group, but also the spirit of his ideas. The warm and playful interactions between the Karmapa and his translator lightened many serious moments, as discussions of grave issues were punctuated by peals of laughter and smiles exchanged all around. Early in the students' time with him, the Karmapa hosted a lunch for them, breaking with protocol by sending the teachers and translator to a separate table, and inviting the students to sit with him to share casual conversation. Setting a tone of warmth and informal engagement, he questioned them about their lives and families—and even asked about one student's dreadlocks.

On their final night in Dharamsala, the group shared another meal with His Holiness, and they took this opportunity to express their gratitude. The students offered him their poems and music, as well as a gift they designed to commemorate their time with him. One song that they sang for His Holiness was "Let the Moon Be the Holder of My Love," an original composition by two of the students that was based on a comment the Karmapa had made in one of his teachings to them (see chapter 3, "Healthy Relationships," page 27). The Karmapa's chant master had graciously taught five of the students a sacred song by the great Tibetan yogi Milarepa. Seated in front of the Karmapa for the last time, the students sang the sacred song to him in Tibetan, using a tune the Karmapa himself had composed. After a few moments, His Holiness joined in, merging his voice with theirs.

Note: The title "His Holiness" might be more familiar when used in Buddhism as a term referring to the most revered of all Tibetan Buddhist teachers, His Holiness the Dalai Lama. This title is often applied to the Karmapa as well, as a measure of the high esteem in which he is held by his millions of followers worldwide.

Editors' Introduction

PEOPLE ALL AROUND THE GLOBE are deeply concerned about the state of the world and wish to change it, yet many feel unsure how to do so or where to begin. In this book, His Holiness the Karmapa orients us toward a more compassionate world, which can be reached through our own efforts. While acknowledging the enormity of the task, he maintains that we already have what we need to create that world in the basic nobility of the human heart.

As the author explores the major interpersonal, social, and environmental issues facing us today, he points out the emotional resources we have that can help us tackle these formidable challenges. He urges us to rigorously consider human goodness as the basis for our work to transform the world. All too aware of the obstacles that can block our access to that basis of goodness within us, the Karmapa demonstrates how such obstacles can be removed. His sustained argument challenges us to rethink our understanding of who we are and what we are truly capable of. The author's vision of how we can make a significant difference in the world is at once simple and profound; it encourages a way of living that is deeply challenging, yet entirely feasible.

This demanding optimism is grounded in the reality of the interdependence of individuals, communities, social systems, and the environment. Recent decades have brought greater awareness of the numberless subtle ties that link disparate phenomena in the world: global warming, labor migration, and international markets evidence the deep connectedness that pervades our physical and social worlds. Although interdependence is increasingly acknowledged in many forms of public discourse, serious consideration of its ethical and practical ramifications has barely begun. His Holiness the Karmapa has much to offer here as he draws on Buddhist schools of thought that have been applying the principle of interdependence to social and ethical issues for more than two millennia. In this book, he deploys interdependence as a highly productive framework for thinking about what it means to be a human being, and how we can contribute to the world around us.

Interdependence implies that the support of others is indispensable for our very survival, as well as everything above and beyond that. This truth is evident all around us: it is experienced in every single meal we eat, since each meal is made possible through contributions from numberless others—other people, animals, and the natural environment itself. His Holiness the Karmapa demonstrates this reality of interdependence in multiple contexts—from environmentalism to social justice and conflict resolution, and from healthy relationships to gender identity. In the process, he reveals the emotional, ethical, and practical implications of interdependence for our life and for our place in the world. An awareness of interdependence can deepen emotional responses of gratitude, empathetic love, and compassion. The Karmapa argues that in ethical terms, receiving so much from others entails a responsibility to contribute back to the planet and the beings that share it with us. Our interdependence also brings extensive practical consequences. Since we are dependent on other people and the environment, we have to concern ourselves with the conditions of their well-being in order to ensure our own happiness.

These perspectives offer a new way to see the world, and more importantly, they create the basis for a new way to act within it. The Karmapa issues a call to action, but this is not an appeal for dramatic gestures or high-visibility activism. Instead, the author shows how using our interdependence wisely and grounding our actions in our noble heart can combine to give even small acts a long reach. Our ordinary life can become extraordinary when compassionate intentions guide all that we do.

In this way, His Holiness the Karmapa recovers a place for heroism in daily life. As we learn to value our own capacity for noble intentions, we begin to make use of any conditions we find in order to engage in heroic and noble endeavors. His perspective offers us a remarkable gift that allows us to measure success by the happiness we create for ourselves and for others. In order for our life to be meaningful, it need not be anything more than it is right now.

Even as the Karmapa calls on us to build the world that we want to inhabit, he consistently reminds us that the renovation work actually starts within. He traces the very real problems we see in the world—including rampant consumerism, religious intolerance, world hunger, and the degradation of the environment—to destructive emotions and habitual attitudes such as greed, anger, and selfishness. In this way, he points out that real social transformation is only possible when it includes personal transformation.

We may come to this book wanting to learn how to change the world, but we soon come to see that the change begins with ourselves—our attitudes, our aspirations, and our emotional responses to the problems we wish to address. While the Karmapa strongly affirms the value of our wish to work for a greater collective good, he gently but consistently shifts us away from a purely outward orientation. In order to be most effective in our work in the world, we need to be willing to look within.

It may be startling for us to see ourselves as the author sees us—as not naturally greedy or aggressive, but possessed of inherent goodness, which lies underneath whatever else may be obscuring this goodness from our view. But as we begin to glimpse what he is seeking to show us, the project the Karmapa proposes comes to seem viable—challenging, yes, but viable and eminently worthwhile. Rather than fearing what we will find lurking in our heart, we gain confidence that if we go deep enough, we will find our way back to our noble heart, which can then become the ground for our actions.

These perspectives on human nature, the reality of interdependence, and the power of compassionate intentions to transform the world, are all developed through common experiences. As His Holiness the Karmapa explains, he has chosen to base his presentation in experience rather than philosophy in order to ensure that we meet on ground we can all share—the ground of shared human experience and shared concerns for the world. For the most part, he avoids Buddhist terminology, which is consistent with his aim in this book not to teach about Buddhism, but to share what Buddhism has helped him discover about life and the world.

This book evolved from a series of sessions with American university students. The Karmapa reached out to them—just as he is now reaching out to readers of this book—across boundaries of culture, language, and social position.

The connection he encourages may be described as a form of friendship that could transform our ideals of how we can best live in a global community. It is a friendship that acknowledges the reality of our interdependence, where the contributions of each person may be different, yet still fully valued. As happens naturally between good friends, even as the Karmapa is encouraging us to think and act differently, he does not ask us to become anything different from what we are.

This book constitutes the Karmapa's invitation to work together toward a shared future. It offers tools for navigating back to our noble heart, and for constructing our diverse ways of living in the world. Everyone is invited to investigate how she or he might employ these tools in their own lives. In this collective project to change the world from the inside out, there is a place for everyone. We are each invited to come as we are, bringing with us our own aspirations for the good of the world.

The Heart Is Noble

1 • Our Shared Ground

INSIDE EACH OF US there is a noble heart. This heart is the source of our finest aspirations for ourselves and for the world. It fills us with the courage to act on our aspirations. Our nobility may be obscured at times, covered over with small thoughts or blocked by confused and confusing emotions. But a noble heart lies intact within each of us nonetheless, ready to open and be offered to the world. Our task—the task of this book—is to recognize this noble heart within us and learn to connect with it, to make it the basis of all that we do and feel. When we clear away all that blocks it, this heart can change the world.

Although I am a Buddhist monk, this is not a book about Buddhist theory or practice, but about our experiences as human beings. The shared ground that we meet on is our concern about our lives and our world. On that ground, we can meet as friends. My formal study has been in Buddhist philosophy and religion, so I may use some Buddhist terms on occasion. But this is only because I have found them helpful in my own life, and hope they might also open up useful perspectives for you. Please do not take my words to be an authoritative representation of what the Buddhist texts say. I really am speaking from my own experience.

I am now twenty-five years old. Since the time I was recognized as the Seventeenth Karmapa when I was very young, I have also been aware that I am carrying the nine-hundred-year-old reincarnation lineage of the previous sixteen Karmapas. But I see myself as a human being, not "the Karmapa." I am just a human being with particular responsibilities and opportunities. I may have a unique role because I received the name and position of "Karmapa," but we all have responsibilities based on what we receive from the world.

Although I have had extensive training in order to meet my duties as Karmapa, my initial spiritual education came from my parents. This may be true for many of us. While my mother cannot read, she is sincere, affectionate, and loving. My mother and father were my first spiritual teachers. Our parents bring us into the world and raise us. No matter where we come from, as young children we were all cared for by someone—by parents or by other guardians. This is an experience we all share.

We also share the same planet. We have been living on it together since we were born. We just had not been introduced to one another before. It is good that we can now meet through this book. This meeting of ours doesn't have to lead anywhere. I will be sharing my aspirations for the world with you in this book. If we recognize that we share many experiences and aspirations, that will be enough.

As we go through our lives, we all experience a great deal of change. Tremendous material progress is taking place everywhere around us, before our very eyes. We have all observed our own bodies growing rapidly from childhood, and as we mature we can watch ourselves continue to evolve. This physical development should be matched by mental development. Along with outer growth, we should also look for a deepening of our wisdom, and our ability to distinguish what is beneficial from what is harmful. Just as we can experience the bloom of our youth physically, we can also have an inner blooming of our heart and mind. We can bring this freshness of youth to the world. Later, we can also bring the ripening of our mature wisdom to it.

As we go through life, there is a great deal we can learn from one another. I have been touched by the genuine aspirations of many of the people I meet. I have learned from them.

I have many hopes for the world, but I try not to have any expectations. Whether I can actually fulfill my aspirations or not, I wish to let them shape me and guide my actions in the world. Focusing on achieving results can make us too attached to our goals. Our dreams do not necessarily have to be fulfilled in order for us to be happy. Nurturing hopes is meaningful in and of itself. It is worth working toward them, regardless of the outcome. When we make this shift away from results, we will find greater courage to act on our aspirations for the world. We will find our nobility of heart.

Until now, we have been sharing this earth without recognizing that fact. Now, we can also share our hopes for our common home. We can have common aspirations for ourselves and for each other. We do not need anything more complicated than that. Sharing aspirations and experiences can bring us together on a basic human level. Just that can bring us happiness.

2 • A Meaningful Life

Anything Is Possible

WHEN YOU ARE DREAMING of what is possible for your life, you should know that anything is possible. You may not always feel it or see it, but you never for a single moment lack the capacity to change course. Your life is subject to infinite revision. In fact, change is the most enduring feature of your existence. The person you are today is not the person you will be in ten years, five years, or even one year. Circumstances around you are continually shifting, and you are constantly responding to those changes in ways that shape you. Not only do you have this infinite freedom to shape yourself all the time, but what you do also helps shape the world around you.

The question is: How do you relate to this infinite ground of possibility that your life is built on? How can you create a meaningful life within whatever shifting circumstances you find yourself?

Buddhist thought devotes a great deal of attention to these questions. The view that life holds infinite possibility is explored using the concepts of "interdependence" and "emptiness." When you first hear the term "emptiness," you might think this suggests nothingness or a void, but actually "emptiness" here should remind us that nothing exists in a vacuum. Everything is embedded within a context—a complex set of circumstances. Those contexts themselves are endlessly shifting. When we say that things are "empty," we mean they lack any independent existence outside of those changing contexts. Because everything and everyone is "empty" in this sense, they are capable of endless adaptation. We ourselves have the basic flexibility to adapt to anything, and to become anything.

Because of this, we should not mistake emptiness for nothingness. On the contrary, emptiness is full of potency. Understood correctly, emptiness inspires optimism, rather than pessimism, because it reminds us of the boundless range of possibilities of who we can become and how we can live.

Interdependence and emptiness show us that there are no fixed starting points. We can start from nothing. Whatever we have, wherever we are—that is the place we can start from. Many people have the idea that they lack what they need in order to start working toward their dreams. They feel they do not have enough power, or they do not have enough money. But they should know that any point is the right starting point. This is the perspective that emptiness opens up. We can start from zero.

In fact, emptiness can be compared to the concept and function of zero. Zero may seem like nothing, but as we all know, everything starts from it. Without zero, our computers would collapse. Without zero, we could not start counting from one up to infinity. In the same way, from emptiness, anything and everything can manifest itself.

Anything can come into being because there is no fixed way for things to be. It all depends on the conditions that come together. But this fact that anything is possible does not imply that life is random or haphazard. We can make anything happen, but we can only do so by bringing together the necessary conditions. This is where the concepts of "emptiness" and "interdependence" come together.

Every person, place, and thing is entirely dependent on others—other people and other things—as a necessary condition for its existence. For example, we are alive right now because we are enjoying the right conditions for our survival. We are alive because of the countless meals we have eaten during our life. Because the sun shines on the earth and the clouds bring rain, crops can grow. Someone tends to the crops and harvests them, someone else brings them to market, and yet another person makes a meal from them that we can eat. Each time this process is repeated, the interdependence of our lives links us with more and more people, and with more and more rays of sun and drops of rain.

Ultimately, there is nothing and no one with whom we are not connected. The Buddha coined the term "interdependence" to describe this state of profound connectedness. Interdependence is the nature of reality. It is the nature of human life, of all things and of all situations. We are all linked, and we all serve as conditions affecting each other.

Amid all the conditions that affect us, in fact, the choices we ourselves make and the steps we take are among the most important conditions that affect what arises from our actions. If we act constructively, what comes into being is constructive. If we act destructively, what results is destructive and harmful. Everything is possible, but also everything we do matters, because the effects of our actions reach far beyond ourselves. For that reason, living in a world of interdependence has very specific implications for us. It means our actions affect others. It makes us all responsible for one another.

Living this Reality

I realize this presentation might initially seem abstract, but emptiness and interdependence are not abstract principles. They are very practical, and have direct relevance when you are thinking about how to create a meaningful life.

You can see interdependence at work by looking at how your own life is sustained. Is it only through your own exertions? Do you manufacture all your own resources? Or do they come from others? When you contemplate these questions, you will see very quickly that you are able to exist only because of others. The clothes you wear and the food you eat all come from somewhere else. Consider the books you read, the cars you ride in, the movies you watch, and the tools you use. Not one of us single-handedly makes any of these things for ourselves. We all rely on outside conditions, including the air we breathe. Our continued presence here in the world is an opportunity made possible entirely by others.

Interdependence means we are continually interacting with the world around us. This interaction works both ways—it is a mutual exchange. We are receiving, but also giving. Just as our presence on this planet is made possible by many factors, our presence here affects others in turn—other individuals, other communities, and the planet itself.

Over the past century, we humans have developed very dangerous capabilities. We have created machines endowed with tremendous power. With the technology available now, we could cut down all the trees on the planet. But if we did so, we could not expect life to go on as before, except without trees. Because of our fundamental interdependence, we would all experience the consequences of such actions very quickly. Without any trees, there would not be enough oxygen in our atmosphere to sustain human life.

You may wonder what this has to do with the choices we make and how we live our life. That is simple: We all need to take interdependence into account because it influences our life directly and profoundly. In order to have a happy life, we must take an active interest in the sources of our happiness.

Our environment and the people we share it with are the main sources of our sustenance and well-being. In order to ensure our own happiness, we have to respect and care about the happiness of others. We can see this in something as simple as the way we treat the people who prepare our food. When we treat them well and look after their needs, only then can we reasonably expect them to take pains to prepare something healthy and tasty for us to eat.

When we have respect for others and take an interest in their flourishing, we ourselves flourish. This can be seen in business as well. When customers have more money to spend, businesses do better. If we wish to flourish individually and together as a society, it is not enough for us to simply acknowledge the obvious interdependence of the world we live in. We must consider its implications, and reflect on the conditions for our own welfare. Where do our oxygen and food and material goods come from, and how are they produced? Are these sources sustainable?

Relating to Reality

Looking at your experience from the perspectives of emptiness and interdependence might entail a significant shift in how you understand your life. My hope is that this shift can benefit you in practical terms. Gaining a new understanding of the forces at work in your life can be a first step toward relating positively to them.

My purpose in raising these issues is certainly not to terrify you by confronting you with harsh reality. For example, I have noticed that some people are uncomfortable when they are told that change is a fundamental part of life, or that nothing lasts forever. Yet impermanence is just a basic fact of our existence—it is neither good nor bad in itself. There is certainly nothing to gain by denying it. In fact, when we face impermanence wisely, we have an opportunity to cultivate a more constructive way of relating to that reality. If we do so, we can actually learn to feel at ease in the face of unexpected change, and work comfortably with whatever new situations might occur. We can become more skillful in how we relate to the reality of change.

The same is true of interdependence. Seeing life from this perspective can help us develop skills to relate more constructively to reality—but just knowing that we are interdependent does not guarantee that we will feel good about being so. Some people may initially find it uncomfortable to reflect that they depend on others. They might think this means they are helpless or trapped, as if they were boxed in by those dependencies. Yet when we think about being interdependent, we do not need to feel it is like being stuck in a job working for a boss that we did not choose but have to deal with, like it or not. That is not helpful. We should not feel reluctant or pressured by the reality of our interdependence. Such an attitude prevents us from having a sense of contentment and well-being within our own life. It does not give us a basis for positive relationships.

Interdependence is our reality, whether we accept it or not. In order to live productively within such a reality, it is better to acknowledge and work with interdependence, wholeheartedly and without resistance. This is where love and compassion come in. It is love that leads us to embrace our connectedness to others, and to participate willingly in the relations created by our interdependence. Love can melt away our defenses and our painful sense of separation. The warmth of friendship and love makes it easy for us to accept that our happiness is intimately linked to that of others. The more widely we are able to love others, the happier and more content we can feel within the relations of interdependence that are a natural part of our life.

All People Are Like Parents to Us

Love is possible in all our relationships because all people want happiness. No one wants to suffer. This is true of the people we love. It is also true of those we dislike. We are all absolutely identical in this respect. I think this universal wish for happiness is something we can easily grasp intellectually. When we learn to also feel and respect this in our heart, love naturally flourishes within us.

Among all the people we are connected to, most of us feel a particular affection and love for our parents. Why? A sense of closeness and love usually arises more easily toward our parents because they have cared for us, helped us grow, and contributed to our well-being.

As I see it, all people are very much like parents to us. If we look carefully, we can see that everyone we meet has contributed to our well-being in a variety of ways, directly or indirectly. Many different people have cooked our meals, and built the shelter and sewn the clothes that protect us from the elements. They have driven us where we wanted to go, and invented medicine that healed us when we were sick. They have educated us, helped us stand on our own feet, challenged us to grow, and much, much more. Countless people have been functioning just like parents to us from the moment we were born until now. But we do not usually recognize others as parents, partly because we have not had our attention drawn to their parent-like qualities. No one steps forward and introduces themselves, saying, "Hi, I'm actually like a mother to you." Nor do we shake their hand, saying, "Hello, you are like a father to me."

But if we really consider all that we receive from others, we can identify endless ways in which many people are like parents to us. When we do, we will approach them with more tenderness. We will be able to connect to them with the same kind of love that exists between a mother and child. We will be able to embrace our interdependence, and happily and joyfully take others' need for happiness to heart. Because everyone wants love, we have the power to improve others' lives by giving them what they want and need—beginning by just feeling love toward them.

Taking a Limitless View

I believe that this wider perspective is essential in thinking about making our life meaningful. What gives life real meaning? That is a vast question. In order to answer it, we need to think in a vast way. We need to see far beyond our own limited life. If we are considering nothing more than our own personal territory and personal concerns, that view is much too myopic.

As an example, in my own life I have had a great number of unfulfilled wishes and can find many reasons to feel dissatisfied. Unlike other people my age, some of the most important choices in my life were made for me by others. This began from the time I was recognized as the Karmapa at the age of seven. On top of having many great responsibilities placed on me as the Karmapa, I have also encountered great challenges and obstacles in fulfilling those duties. Of course, it can be frustrating not to be able to do everything I want to do and am required to do. But this does not make my life meaningless or hopeless. It is up to me to decide how to meet these challenges and obstacles.

The idea that life is meaningless if one's wishes are not fulfilled is the result of narrow thinking. It is a sign of thinking only of oneself, and a very narrow sense of oneself at that. Even when life seems meaningless because our particular wishes are not fulfilled, we still have limitless possibilities. We can see that this is so because our life reaches far beyond where we find ourselves at any given moment.

Our life is vast. It does not stop at the limits of what we personally experience. It is not something concrete or bounded. I do not think it is valid to view our life as limited to just ourselves—as if our human life extended only as far as our own body. Rather, we can see that a life extends out in all directions, like a net. We throw a net, and it expands outward. Just like that, our life extends to touch many other lives. Our life can reach out and become a pervasive part of everyone's life.

I believe that our life can only seem meaningless when we think of it in a limited way, as just what is linked to us directly. Personally, if I were to look at my own life in that way, it could all seem pretty pointless. Bearing this big name, escaping from Tibet, all the efforts made since then—it would hardly be worth so much fuss for just one person—me! But when I see my life as something expansive, and see that I might be able to bring some happiness and joy to even just one other person, then I know that my life has real meaning.

You offer joy and happiness to another person, and it reflects back into your own life. The meaningfulness of your life does not come from you as a separate individual. It does come from you, but only through your connectedness to others. In this way, your interrelatedness can give great meaning to your life.

The trick is to strike the right balance between what you want for yourself and what you want for others. To achieve that balance, from the outset what you want for yourself must be well-thought-out. By this I mean that if what you want for yourself is strongly self-centered, you will find no real balance. This is because you are just one part of your life. Since that is so, you must necessarily take others into consideration. Your own interests and your own life will only be balanced when they include both the well-being of yourself and others. Any wholesome undertaking necessarily includes a desire to benefit others. If an undertaking is egocentric and full of self-cherishing, then that balance will be extremely difficult to find and maintain. You need to care for yourself, of course, but not to the total disregard of others. Your accomplishments cannot come at the expense of others.

Three Kinds of Aims

If we think about what generally guides our pursuits, we can see that some aims are entirely self-interested. Other goals combine our own interests with the interests of others, and still others are pursued entirely for the benefit of others. There is a big difference in our experiences, based on which sort of aim we are pursuing—self-interested, altruistic, or a combination of the two.

When we care only about our own interests, we end up neglecting other people and even showing contempt for them. That basic attitude is: "If they're happy, fine. If they suffer, fine—as long as I get my needs met." This is not only unfortunate; it is entirely out of step with reality. This approach will not work. Because all beings are interdependent, the pursuit of even the most self-centered aims inevitably involves and impacts others. Common sense should tell us that total self-interest is self-defeating.

The second kind of aim—when our own interests are joined with the interests of others—recognizes our interdependence. Here, the attitude is: "I want to meet my goals, and of course, at the same time others should be able to meet theirs, too. Just as I'm pursuing my aims, I hope their personal aims can be met, too." If we want to take care of ourselves, then we have to respect that same wish in others, too.

The third sort of aim involves seeking only others' interests. This altruism can be much harder to feel, much less put into practice. When we cherish only others' wishes and goals, we willingly sacrifice our own aims if we see that doing so benefits others. We should not take this to mean that we literally give up our life, or that we never have any of our own needs met. Rather, it is a mental outlook in which we are willing to forgo our own needs. It is a noble approach in which we orient our life entirely to the service of others. This might be hard for us to translate into immediate action, but it is an attitude we can aspire to.

Cherishing Self and Others

I'll share two stories as examples of pursuing one's own versus others' aims. The first is of a two-headed eagle; let's call it an American bald eagle. This eagle had two heads. We know from biology that each head naturally has its own brain, but this two-headed, two-brained eagle had only one body. (Sorry, this is funny science, I know!) The two heads had different ways of seeing the world, and they didn't much care for each other. In fact, they each really wanted the whole body to themselves. Each head started scheming ways to get rid of the other.

One day, this two-headed bird landed near some poison. Each

of the heads leapt at this opportunity to do away with the other. Each tried to entice the other to eat the poison, describing how delicious it was and courteously inviting the other to treat himself to it. Finally one of the heads—the less persuasive one, I guess—gobbled up the poison. But of course, this act poisoned the whole body that they shared. They were each so focused on their own self-centered aims and their dislike of one another that they forgot that they shared the same body.

This is what happens when we are self-absorbed. In the end, we only harm ourselves. To have a meaningful life, we must see our life as an integral part of a much larger whole. Given the reality of our tightly interconnected existence in this world, it is absolutely reasonable to say that we are all sharing one life. We have many heads, but one body.

The second story is of a house that caught on fire with a whole family inside. One member of the family panicked, and bolted for the nearest way out of the house. His first thought was his own self-preservation, and he managed to make it safely to the door. But just as his front foot made it past the threshold, he suddenly remembered his family. He kept his back foot inside the door, with the feeling that he wanted the same life and safety for his family that he was rushing to secure for himself. After stopping for that split second with his balance evenly distributed between the two feet, he immediately turned to go back in order to save the others.

We need to act in a similar way. That leading foot points to where we want to go ourselves, while the other foot reminds us that others want that same thing for themselves, too. We need to create the possibility of having both these feet on the ground. Our self-interest can tell us what we want for ourselves, but our awareness of others reminds us that they want it, too. We should not sacrifice ourselves entirely, or run ourselves down for others to the point of self-deprivation. Nor should we disregard others for the sake of our own well-being. This is the right balance.

Meaningful Livelihood

Once you have a clear sense of the balance that makes life meaningful, then you will be in a good position to think about choosing a particular livelihood, and integrating your work into the rest of your life.

The particular profession or job you do is not the most important factor. My job is to be Karmapa, and that is a pretty tough job—tough to do, and even tough to describe. In the space for occupation in a passport, what should I write? Reciter of prayers? That's too narrow. Tree planter? That sounds strange. Cook? I don't know how to cook, so that is out. I guess I am many things and nothing, but the main point is not what you do, but how you do it.

Whatever work you do, you have to give yourself opportunities to just be. Even if it is only once a day, you should find a moment to just be yourself in the course of each day. This could be through a short period of meditation or quiet reflection in the morning or in the evening, or in whatever way best suits you. The point is to reconnect with yourself. Otherwise, the whole day you are running around and busy, and it is easy to lose yourself. To guard against this, you should make efforts to return to yourself and recollect what is essential for you.

Letting your job drive you can become dehumanizing. I have some acquaintances who work in factories, and they have to calibrate themselves to the machines. In their daily lives, they become like robots themselves. In other jobs too, people adjust the rhythm of their lives to the rhythm of their jobs. This is deeply distressing. It is an extreme example of the dangers of making ourselves part of an economic system that treats people like machines.

Such examples might make it seem attractive to drop out of the system and seek some alternatives. Yet for those of us who feel a deep commitment to changing a particular system, or contributing to shaping our world for the better, there are some other factors to consider. While there may be exceptions, when we choose to move outside of a system, this often amounts to little more than running away—even when we leave with the idea that we will oppose the system from outside. It easily becomes like discarding something we do not like, instead of trying to repair or modify it. We see examples of people who leave one system and then the next, creating a pattern of escape. This is not an effective way to reform the system. In order to bring change, though it may be difficult, working within the system can have a far greater effect.

Where Real Worth Lies

Whether you work within a system or outside it, I would like to emphasize that it is a mistake to link your identity to the work you do. No job can ever define you as a person. You are so much more than your job. No matter how many hours a day you spend working, it is not the only or even the most important part of your life. At most, it can be one component within the vast net of all that comprises your human life.

This is particularly important to keep in mind in this difficult economic climate. When people lose their jobs nowadays, they might not find a new one quickly. Some unemployed people suffer terribly due to the emotional costs of being jobless, even more than they suffer from lack of income. If your job is filling an emotional hole, that hole will remain painfully open while you are jobless. You can counteract such feelings by refreshing your understanding of where happiness truly comes from. With all of our intelligence, we often fall back into a mistaken habit of seeking happiness in external things and circumstances. You can refresh your wise awareness and, at any moment, you can turn your attention from outer conditions to the inexhaustible source of goodness you have inside yourself. That can never be lost, no matter what the situation.

We let ourselves be delighted by gaining new material possessions. Why shouldn't we let ourselves be much more delighted with our own inner goodness? It is worth so much more. Our personal qualities can make us happy. We just have to turn our attention to them.

Giving rise to a single moment of cherishing others can bring us much deeper satisfaction than making money. Our own positive qualities can be rich sources of joy for us. Even if we have just one altruistic thought, this is a cause to be deeply happy. We have ample resources for happiness in the bounty of our own mind.

3 • Healthy Relationships
Orienting Ourselves toward Others

N O MATTER WHAT is going on around us, we always have
ways to make our life deeply meaningful for ourselves and
for others. All it takes is a shift in perspective. Recalling the principle of interdependence, we can expand our sense of ourselves
beyond the narrow limits of our own body and experiences, to encompass everything our life connects to. Then we can look beyond
our own aims, and embrace others' goals as our own.

When we bring our concern for ourselves into harmony with
our concern for others, our life comes into balance. When our life
feels imbalanced and pointless, usually we notice that our relationships have also become unhealthy. By thinking carefully about
how we orient ourselves toward others and toward ourselves, we
can build and enjoy healthy relationships. We can learn to cultivate relationships that are warm and truly meaningful.

Although Buddhist philosophy and psychology offer extensive discussions of relationships, I want to approach this topic
through experience rather than through theory. I think focusing
on emotions helps us address our experiences—the way we actually feel and live our relationships.

I have observed that emotional bonds are formed between
people to a large degree by force of habit—that is, by becoming
familiar with each other in particular ways. I think it is worth

paying more attention to the role of habitual patterns in our relationships, because by forming new habits, we can fundamentally change the way we relate to others. For example, two people are brought together through repeated association, and in the process each becomes accustomed to the other. They relate to each other again and again in a similar way, and slowly come to feel comfortable with each other and with the patterns of their relationship. That is often all it takes to form an emotional bond—and to establish patterns that will be followed in their future interaction.

The Buddhist way of explaining this envisions a long series of actions that extend back to our previous lives, and that come to form habitual patterns that are brought into our present life with us. But we need look no further than our present life to see that dynamics from our early years recur much later in life. This happens because we gravitate toward relationships that feel familiar somehow, based on patterns that emerged earlier. Simple habituation also contributes a great deal to our sense of what feels comfortable culturally.

But habits can be changed. We can come to feel comfortable in new environments once we get used to them. Habits are only formed through sheer repetition over time, so by repeatedly acting in new ways, we can create new habits and break old ones. To do this, we can begin by examining our usual ways of thinking and relating. When we have determined that we need to cultivate healthier habits in our relationships, we can take care to consistently approach others in a healthier way, until the new approach is established as a habitual response—a positive one.

The Fabricated "I"

The force of habit also plays a subtle but important role in the way we see ourselves. Our sense of ourselves in turn has a tremendous impact on the way we relate to others. We can speak of two senses of ourselves, or two forms of "I." One is an innate or instinctual "I," and the other "I" is imputed or learned through our customary way of viewing ourselves.

I should explain what I mean by these two senses of "I" that we all feel. I will start with the latter, which is less subtle, and therefore easier to see at work in our life. This "I"—the learned or imputed "I"—is constructed or fabricated through repeated use, so I will call it the fabricated "I." Your parents tell you that you are like this or like that. Your teachers at school tell you that you are like this or like that. The concepts of gender in your society tell you what you should be like. Your culture in general sends you many messages about who you are.

I understand that there is a tendency in American culture to boost children's confidence by telling them how important and special they are. That self-understanding also becomes part of this fabricated sense of self. The "I" comes to seem increasingly real and solid as you grow habituated to thinking of yourself as the person you are told you are at home, at school, and within your larger social world. This is the fabricated "I." Your own mental habits lead you to think that this is really who you are, and this fabricated "I" then constitutes a sense of self that you carry with you everywhere you go in life, and through all your relationships.

By contrast, the other sense of self—the innate one—is extremely subtle. Under normal circumstances, we are largely unaware of its presence, although it is always there with us. This subtle sense of self only really becomes manifest or perceptible in certain extreme situations, such as when our life comes under threat. For example, if we suddenly find ourselves on the edge of a cliff about to fall off, that instinctual feeling of an "I" that we urgently want to keep safe would be an expression of this innate sense of "I."

Of the two "I"s, it is the fabricated "I" that takes on great importance in our relationships. For example, no one is born as "Jack." Rather, someone gets named "Jack," and with that act, the person "Jack" is created. Then he grows up thinking: "I am

Jack. Jack—that's me." Later, if someone speaks badly of "Jack," he is shaken and agitated. He can be in a room with a hundred other people, but if someone calls out the name "Jack," he feels completely singled out and put on the spot. No matter how many other people are there, the sound of the word "Jack" seems targeted directly at him. This is a sign that he has taken ownership of the label "Jack." He takes whatever is said of this "Jack" terribly seriously and personally, because he has taken that identity upon himself. We all do this.

You believe that your fabricated "I" is naturally you, and correctly reflects your complete and true identity. But if you contemplate the process, you can actually see that your fabricated "I" was gradually built up over a period of time. You became so familiar with it that you now think it is inherently who you are. But it is not. It is just a constructed identity.

Nevertheless, the sense of self that this fabricated "I" gives you, and the sense of "mine" that comes along with it, create a sort of window through which you view the world. You sit inside looking out through this frame of "I" and "mine," and then you take whatever you see through that window personally. If someone outside has an angry expression, you feel that this person's anger must be directed at you. In reality, there is no reason to accept someone else's experience of anger as being connected to you. After all, they are also looking out from their own personal window, and their perceptions are also fundamentally rooted in their own sense of "I."

When we gaze out through our own window of grasping at "me" and "mine," we experience everything as if it were being projected onto our personal frame of perception, like a movie projected onto a screen. Just as when we are watching a movie, if we observe a happy moment, our heart soars, and if there is a sad moment, we at once feel low.

This grasping at "me" and "mine" restricts our view of ourselves. It also severely impacts how we connect to others. It prevents us from seeing the numberless wholesome connections that truly link us to others. We end up relating to the world as if it were separate from us, something out there projected on a screen for our consumption. I am not presenting a philosophical view here. I am trying to describe what it feels like to experience the world this way. As we look out through our window, we feel attachment and aversion. We accept or reject what we see projected on the screen. This emotional push and pull forms a major component of how we relate to others.

The Hook of Attachment

The wish to pull in or push away what we perceive around us is a big force in our relationships. Rather than relaxing and appreciating the other person, we engage in a constant struggle to get what we want from them, and to avoid getting what we do not want. For that reason, in order to build healthy relationships we need to deal with our attachment as well as our aversion.

. It might be useful to start by looking at our assumptions about attachment and also about nonattachment. Conventional wisdom leads many people to question whether or not relationships are even possible without attachment. I have heard people say that if there were no attachment, they would have no close relationships. People try to induce attachment in others as a basis for starting a relationship with them. They wield attachment like a hook, trying to pull people toward them and literally get them hooked.

If you find it hard to imagine how a warm and healthy relationship could exist in the absence of attachment, this indicates confusion between being detached and being free of attachment. Detachment is very different from nonattachment. Detachment suggests an unfeeling indifference. By contrast, when there is an absence of attachment, healthy feelings have ample room to blossom. This is because attachment causes you to be totally consumed by something or someone. For example, you cannot stop thinking about someone you met who you feel sure will make your life perfect. Your mental space is completely occupied, and you may be so overtaken by thoughts of this person that you can hardly think of anything else. It can seem as if all your thinking has already been done for you. You just follow along under the spell of your attachment, like a small insect stuck in honey, unable to get away.

We become overwhelmed by difficult external situations just as we become overwhelmed by our own attachment. For example, when we encounter problems in life, we may feel that circumstances are surrounding us on all sides and driving us in directions we did not choose. Both in the case of working with attachment and of working with difficult situations, the challenge for us is to figure out how to steer things ourselves. For that, we need to be able to find new ways to think about our situation.

When we feel overcome by a situation, although it may be true that the situation is there all around us, we can still mentally lift ourselves above it, and take a second look from that new perspective. For example, if we feel as if we are flailing in the water and drowning in a problem, we can try to imagine ourselves sitting on a mountaintop and surveying our situation in the valley below. This gives us a different way of seeing things, and can reveal new options for responding.

I am not suggesting that you shut down emotionally or disengage from the situation. Of course, you remain connected and engaged. But if you are able to mentally come out from the middle of it all, you can view your situation from a different angle. You create a sort of second you, and you find a second angle of vision that offers a new way of thinking. Nonattachment does not mean parting from someone or failing to fully engage in a relationship. Rather, it is a shift in your perspective that gives you a more open view.

Given all the pain and confusion our attachments cause us, it is curious how difficult it is for us to see that attachment itself is a problem. I have thought about this a lot, and it seems to me that one reason why we find it hard to recognize that our attachment is problematic is because we have such a strong tendency to look for faults outside of ourselves. We habitually turn outward to assign responsibility for our problems, and tend to blame our unhappiness on external factors. "Where is the problem? It is out there!" When our objects of attachment fail to make us happy, we see the fault as lying in the objects of our attachment, rather than in the feeling of attachment that is rooted within us.

Nevertheless, attachment is a serious problem—and it is a problem we create by ourselves. It is also something we create for ourselves, in the sense that our attachments are ostensibly aimed at our own self-gratification and at serving our own purposes. Attachment is based in self-interest. For example, we do not generally approach the people we are attached to primarily in terms of their well-being. When you get right down to it, we are more interested in how they make us feel and what we get from them.

This becomes apparent when things become unsatisfactory within a relationship of attachment—the blame is always placed on the other person. There is a feeling of "Why do I need to change? He (or she) should be the one to change. He (or she) is the one causing the trouble." This would not be the case if we were truly concerned with the welfare of the other person. If their happiness were our main concern, we would genuinely wish to adapt ourselves in ways that would benefit them. But that is not how we act when attachment is driving us. In fact, attachment is selfish, through and through.

When you truly love someone, they are extremely precious to you—as valuable to you as your own life. You cherish them even more than yourself. But when you are attached to people, you see them as existing in your life to fill your needs or to make you happy. Some men get upset when they see their wives talking to other men, and vice versa. This is really strange, if you think about it. Why should anyone want to prevent their loved one from talking to other people? This wish to control the other person's actions is selfish, and indicates a concern only with one's own wishes and aims. It is a sign that the relationship is based primarily in attachment rather than love.

Love as a Practice

When we come out from behind the window of "me" and "mine" that our fabricated "I" places between ourself and others, our relationships can appear to us in a completely different light. We stop engaging with others on the basis of what they can do for us. We are relieved of the constant desire to pull some people toward us and keep others away. We can instead see multiple ways to connect positively with everyone. From this wide and open perspective, it becomes possible to deepen our love.

When we look at our usual understanding of love, we may find that we often bring some rather wild expectations to it. People speak of enduring or unchanging love. You have the phrase in English, "Until death do us part," and we say something similar in Tibetan. I have some friends who really believe in this. Yet we also see in our relationships that love evolves as circumstances evolve. Because times change, love changes, too.

We resist recognizing this in our relationships. Instead, people think their love relationships will always be fabulous, and that this one will be the best ever. Many people talk to me about their experiences, and I have noticed that in the beginning, they seem to find everything about the new relationship terribly exciting. People call each other every day, and every conversation is completely fascinating. There is an expectation that things will always remain at that same high pitch of intensity. But in time, and especially after people make a long-term commitment, they tend to lose interest. The "undying love" loses its luster. I've even heard people say that marriage is the graveyard of love!

Despite all of this, I believe that love can be lasting. For example, in my own case, I believe that the love I have for all of you does not have to diminish. Love can have an enduring quality when we make it a conscious spiritual practice—but not a spiritual practice in the sense of saying some prayers or doing a little daily meditation. Love is a huge and expansive practice, a great and noble practice.

We actively nurture our love by working wholeheartedly on ourselves. This is the way our own spiritual practice can become a condition that helps love to last. Spiritual practice means transforming ourselves. It means changing. We cannot hope to just find love and keep it on a shelf—as if I have given you my love, you have given me your love, and now we just have to brush the dust off it from time to time, and we are basically done. Contrary to this, love is a living thing. Like a tree, it needs to grow continually, yielding fresh cycles of leaves and flowers and fruit. If this stops, the tree stagnates and eventually dies. Once we embrace love as a fully active practice, only then can we begin to speak of undying love.

Love That Lasts

I have heard it said that if there is a reason to love someone, then it is not really love. There are many ordinary reasons that people point to when explaining why they love someone. Some people say it is the other person's looks. Some say it is the person's personality, or the way the person looks at them. I have even heard that people can fall in love with someone because of the color of his or her hair! Yet if the reason for love is superficial, then it clearly will not last.

The reason and the meaning of love in our life is very profound. It is unlike any other reason. In my own personal view, I do not think that love has to be for no reason at all. Rather, I think that the reason to love is so vast that it cannot be limited to any particular reasons.

Relationships can last, but they do change—sometimes for the better, but sometimes for the worse. Even in a relationship as fundamental and enduring as the relationship between parents and children, things can get so bad that people no longer talk to each other. It can get to the point that they hurt each other physically or verbally. Some parents and children even kill one another. Yet one thing that cannot change is that they are parent and child. The fact of their being related in this way never changes. Even when the particular shape of such a relationship evolves, the essence of their relatedness does not. Placing love at the very heart or essence of a relationship is a way to make it last.

The point I want to make is that love can be true and lasting, under the right conditions. This is my own personal view on this. Love can have this vast, all-encompassing quality. It can be allowed to spread until it permeates the very core of our relationships. Yet often, instead of giving love room to expand, we box it in with our expectations. Expectations make our love conditional on what the other person does or says. Our concern for the other person also becomes conditional on whether or not the relationship fulfills our wishes. How can you expect love to last when you demand that it meet your conditions, and you act as if you own another person? For love to last, it is best not to have too many expectations. It is better just to offer love.

I want to share with you a feeling I have. I feel that my love does not have to remain within the limitations of my own life or body. I imagine that if I am no longer in the world, my love could still be present. I want to place my love on the moon and let the moon hold my love. Let the moon be the keeper of my love, offering it to everyone just as the moon sends its light to embrace the whole earth.

Love Is Essential

Love can sustain us in life, when it is viewed in the right way. It seems to me that many people approach their love relationships as sources of enjoyment or pleasure, whereas they treat their job as a matter of absolute necessity. We have basic needs for food, clothing, and shelter, and so we see practical reasons to keep a job. This view can lead us to believe that jobs are serious business, while somehow relationships are just for fun.

When we approach our life in this way, we end up treating our emotions and relationships as things that are dispensable. It seems that many people are more at ease changing partners than changing jobs. They put up with a great deal of unhappiness and hardship at work, because they see their job as essential to their lives, and not as an optional luxury. But if a partner or friend is too much trouble and does not make them happy, they feel they can just discard them and find a new one later when they get the chance. This comes from holding to the view that love is a dispensable part of our life.

We may want to do away with a problematic relationship, without addressing the underlying cause of those problems—in our own mind and heart. There is a Tibetan saying: "You are angry with the yak, but you whip the horse." This reminds us how ridiculous it is to respond only to things that are not the real cause of our unhappiness. Love and emotional well-being rest within us, not outside of us. Therefore, in order to develop real love and to have healthy relationships, there is no way out of it: we need to probe our own mind and heart.

True love can sustain us when we learn to approach it in the right way. In order for love to be lasting and wholesome, the place to begin is by seeing the wholesome potential we have within our mind and heart. We should know both the faults and the good qualities that lie within us. This means recognizing the capacity for real love that we have, and facing the attachment and hatred that we may also have. The capacity for lasting love rests within our heart, but so do the obstacles to loving well: our self-centered habits, our attachment, our aversion, and our expectations.

Being at Ease with Change

As we probe within ourselves to find the basis for healthy relationships, we see that our own ideas about love can create obstacles. Along with the idea that love should be everlasting comes an unrealistic expectation that we will always be together with the object of our love. Here the issue is not so much that we might lose our own feelings of love, but rather that the relationship itself can be brought to an end by death or by separation.

There is an important distinction between a relationship ending and love ending. Our love for a person can, and very often does, survive the end of our active relationship with them. However, the end of a relationship can be made painful simply by the fact that we are unprepared to accept that it is over. Even with all of our intelligence, somehow we often do not consider the fact that friendships and partnerships will all eventually come to an end, either with the death of one member or with a voluntary separation.

When either of these two things happen, we suffer because we harbored expectations that reality could not meet—in this case, the reality of impermanence. Birth, sickness, and death are inescapable; we cannot keep them from happening. Yet we cling to whatever we like about our current situation—our health, youth, or relationships—wanting and desperately hoping that it will continue indefinitely. Meanwhile, change is the most constant feature in our life. Theoretically, we know we will all die at some point, but we do our best to ignore the inevitability of death. The only way to escape death is to prevent birth, since everything that is born will eventually die. But preventing birth is utterly out of the question for us. Obviously, we have already been born. Since birth and death are natural pairs in this sense, we are bound to die.

These can be very hard facts to face, I know. But denying them can cause us a great deal of pain. It can leave us emotionally vulnerable when things do come to an end, as they inevitably will. Uncomfortable as it may seem, accepting the facts of this reality puts us in a much better position to face major changes in our life wisely.

For many people, the death of a loved one is the most painful experience of their lives. Personally, I also find it difficult. When someone I know dies, I feel that a part of me is missing. I have lost something that was part of me. There is no denying these real feelings of pain that we experience when we lose a loved one.

Different cultures have their own ways of facing a loved one's death. Your culture may tell you that this is a time to grieve. You may feel obligated or somewhat encouraged to give yourself over to grief and pain. Yet there will come a moment to find a new, more constructive response. When that happens, you can recall that the focus of your grief is the person you loved, and perhaps that same person and your love for them can relieve that sorrow. Actually grief is rooted in the feeling of separation from that person you feel affection for—the feeling of having lost him or her. You feel pain because you loved them. Yet that love connects you to them still, although they are gone. This continuity of love can also shape your response to losing them in positive ways.

I find it helpful in these situations to contemplate that I had affection for that person, and they had affection for me. You might also try reflecting in this way: "They wished for my happiness and tried to bring it about. Even as they were dying, that person surely kept with them their hope that I would be happy. They certainly did not want me to suffer. Even after they have gone, their aspirations continue, and I can still work to fulfill those aspirations. Their hopes will now live on as part of me." If you truly adopt this perspective, you can remain deeply connected to the person through your efforts to honor their aspirations for you. All your efforts to live a wise and happy life can become a way to let them continue caring for you even now. In this way, the love they had for you, and you for them, can live on.

If at times you feel yourself slipping back into sadness, you can remind yourself that your loved one's wish for you had been for you to be happy, every day, and not to suffer. If you allow yourself to drown in grief, you dash their hopes for you. If you can ease your own pain, you are bringing their pain to an end too, through the bond of love and hope that still links you to them.

When People Part Ways

Likewise, when it is a separation or breakup that ends a relationship, you can reflect that this too is simply the natural outcome of impermanence. You shouldn't be shocked or surprised at all, even if you feel pain for some time. Change is an integral and inevitable part of life. You can acknowledge that fact, and reflect that change is not necessarily always bad, even if you yourself did not choose it.

In fact, under certain conditions, we do embrace impermanence and actually enjoy it. We watch the seasons change, and have no difficulty appreciating this beauty. As summer's time of flowering comes to an end, the leaves of the trees turn orange and yellow. Next comes the time when the wind carries off all the leaves, and then we have the stark beauty of the bare branches. These changes are a natural part of the rhythm of life. Each phase brings fresh forms of beauty.

When two people separate, there can likewise be freshness and room for new growth. There is a freedom from stagnation. Impermanence can bring many possibilities. (We might even be able to take wry comfort in the fact that we have been relieved of a relationship that had become problematic or burdensome, at least for one of the two partners!)

Even if we do not feel that the separation is good for us, it may be good for the other person. Out of the love and affection we have for the other person, we should consider their contentment and well-being. If there is a concern for the other's happiness that comes from the heart, then a physical separation does not mean a separation from your love for them. Even if you do not meet or speak with someone, you can still maintain your affection and love for them.

I have observed a strange idea of love that many people seem to have: they see love as a kind of gift that has to be given back. Someone says, "I love you," and if the other person does not reply with an "I love you, too," the first person gets upset. But love doesn't always have to be reciprocated. We can just love. If love doesn't come back to you, it is still love that you give and that you feel. We do not always have to look to get something back for what we give, do we?

This is how I see it myself, but I have observed that most people find unrequited love and the end of relationships very hard emotionally. Yet reflecting on impermanence and shifting the focus to the other's welfare are two ways we can maintain equilibrium even in the face of these difficult experiences.

The Place of Projections

Earlier, I spoke of the impact that our fabricated identities have on our relationships. We also fabricate identities for others, projecting images onto them that then affect what we see in them and how we relate to them. Such mental elaborations can create major barriers between people.

I would like to share with you an example from my own life. When I was fourteen years old, I escaped from Tibet. My traveling companions and I had to cross the mountains illegally, and we were utterly terrified of the Chinese police. I remember they wore hats with a very particular shape, a bit like saddles. Just the shape of those hats could fill us with fear.

On our way to the Nepalese border, we had to pass two Chinese army camps. The first one was the most dangerous, because even if we managed to elude capture there, if the soldiers became aware of our presence, they could phone ahead to the next checkpoint and we would be caught there. We had to wait in the car for hours on a very cold winter night, because we had arrived at 10:00 P.M. and could not continue until the guards were asleep. The others in the car with me were telling me to try to get some rest. But how could I sleep? We were all full of this terrible fear of the Chinese soldiers. At one point, we thought we heard something knocking on the door, but we looked outside and there was no one there. We were so scared that we started imagining things, and made ourselves even more terrified.

It was clear this was not helpful. I had to come up with another method to get through this experience. So finally I told myself, "These Chinese soldiers are also human beings. They are not monsters or demons, nor do they have all the qualities we are imputing to them. We could talk to them; they are human like us."

With these thoughts, I started to calm down. Of course, we were in a highly vulnerable position, but by adding my own projections to the actual dangers of the situation, I was making things even worse for myself than they already were.

This may be an extreme example, but it illustrates my point that we fabricate identities for others as well as for ourselves, and these projections clearly color our relationships to others. As I experienced on the way from Tibet, the identities that we ourselves manufacture and project on to others can even prevent us from seeing them as fully human!

One powerful way to improve our relationships is to learn to recognize and drop our own unhelpful projections. We need to do this so we can see the other person more clearly, and accept them more fully as they are. In other words, healthy relationships involve an element of acceptance, or what we can call patience.

Training in Patience

Patience is the wisdom that enables us to be accommodating. Patience does not mean forcing ourselves to put up with things we do not like, or just holding our resentment inside and storing it up. It certainly does not mean staying passive in the face of harm. Rather, patience involves an active application of wise reasoning in order to intentionally dissolve any resentment we might harbor toward others.

The classic example used in Buddhist teachings is to ask ourselves: If someone beats us with a stick, do we get mad at the stick that hit us? If we analyze the situation, we have to acknowledge that it makes more sense to get angry at the hand that wields the stick. Yet it is the mind that directs that hand. And the mind in turn is acting under the influence of anger. Ultimately, it is the anger that moves the stick. This reminds us that the real fault lies in the anger. When we reflect in this way, it becomes clear that we cannot reasonably direct our resentment at the person. We can only justifiably be angry at the anger itself.

The point here is certainly not to let people hit us with sticks! The point is that we are using our reasoning to deconstruct the identities we have fabricated for people. Even in the case of people whose actions seem to demand that we see them in only one way, we can still use our reasoning to expand our view of them. To that end, it is extremely helpful to distinguish the person from their actions, and from the emotional upheavals that happen to be overpowering them at any given moment. When we do so, we can learn to see others as victims of their own emotions, and respond not with fear or anger, but with compassion and with the wisdom of patience. In this way, patience gives us more options in how we relate and respond to others.

Parting with Faults

As long as we are human, we will inevitably make mistakes. Until we learn to completely master our own unruly emotions, we will harm each other and ourselves, too. It is important, therefore, that we find constructive ways to respond to the unfortunate situations that arise in our relationships. Patience allows us to relate constructively with the mistakes of others when they occur. Along with patience, forgiveness of past mistakes is integral to healthy relationships. Forgiveness gives the other person space to grow and move on from their mistakes.

At the same time, it is clear that the faults never lie exclusively on one side of a relationship. For this reason, if we are serious about forging relationships that work, we must also recognize our own faulty attitudes, and work on them. When we commit to identifying our own faults and transforming our own mind, then and only then are healthy relationships possible.

I have noticed that some people can be very critical of themselves. When people have low self-esteem or a tendency to judge themselves harshly, there is a danger that confronting their own faults can just end up reinforcing an unhealthy self-image. A negative fabricated identity can come to seem even more real and solid, and this makes it harder for people to transform. For such people in particular, but also for many of us in general, it is wiser to face our own faults within an overall spirit of forgiveness. Within relationships as well as within our own life, we need space to grow and learn from our mistakes. To that end, forgiving ourselves as well as others is a powerful tool for change.

I would like to offer some suggestions for learning to forgive ourselves by developing a personal practice of what we might loosely call confession. Some Christian and Buddhist traditions include formal confession as a spiritual practice. The word in Tibetan that we use for confession also means "to part" or "to separate." Confession in the Tibetan understanding involves separating ourselves from harmful, negative activity. I think this broad idea of confession could be adopted by people outside a religious context as well.

For example, if we have lied, confessing could involve openly disclosing what we have done, and acknowledging that we recognize that it was wrong. In traditional confession, this admission would be made in front of a religious authority. But I think we could adapt this based on our personal situation. We could admit our mistakes directly to the person we harmed, or we could do so to a trusted friend or another third party. I even think we could go out alone into nature, and make our confession by speaking to the trees or a passing breeze or the sky.

However we make our verbal declaration, the key point is that we do not simply consider the matter closed with mere words. Rather, we also generate the feeling: "That was wrong. Such actions are harmful, and I don't want to have anything to do with them any longer. I never want to do that again, ever. Let me get as far away from these actions as I can. I'm going to be a new person now." In this way, we distance ourselves from harmful behavior, or "separate" ourselves from it. This helps us to make a fresh start as a sort of new person who has parted ways with the earlier person who did the harm. We recognize that the action does not define who we are. We can see for ourselves that we can leave it behind and become a different person.

The point is to create the conditions to make an authentic break with our mistakes. This will not happen if we simply engage in confession as something rote or formulaic. If we go to our temple or church, utter some words, but then come home carrying the same heavy baggage, this does not fulfill the purpose of confessing. Once you have made the sincere and heartfelt determination to leave that conduct behind, there is no longer any need for self-reproach. You do not need to return and revisit your memories of the wrong you did as that old person. You have finished with it.

Harboring a sense of guilt does no good to anybody. "I am so bad, I'm full of faults, I'm a terrible person"—if we are going to cling to these thoughts about ourselves and identify ourselves with our mistakes, then there is little point in confessing before the Buddha or anyone else. Holding on to a negative fabricated identity or self-image, recollecting our past mistakes, and wallowing more deeply in guilt and remorse—this just makes us more stuck in negative ways of thinking and acting.

This misses the point of what a personal practice of confession can offer us. Confession involves transformation: you make a resolve to change. This is something you need to do yourself; no one else can do it for you. Confession is the separation of the past from the future. You confess and then let go, so you can move on without repeating the mistake.

Forgiving Others

I believe cultivating a practice of confessing and forgiving yourself can be a way of training yourself to forgive others. Among the mistakes that others have made, some of their mistakes may have hurt or harmed you. You want them to cease that behavior toward you, and in some ways your forgiveness can help them leave those patterns of behavior behind, and move on to become a new person, too, just as your own confession did for you. It does not mean that you condone their past behavior; it means you want to help create a future in which they no longer behave that way. Just as the practice of confession can help you see that your own mistaken actions do not define you as a person, so you can also distinguish between the other's harmful behavior and the person themselves.

In order to forgive someone who has harmed you, it helps to reflect that the person was certainly driven by some upheaval of strong emotions. The logic we used in asking who really controls the stick can help here. People's crazy emotions can make them act crazily, and you might even see them as suffering from a case of temporary insanity. When people fall into the grip of strong emotions, they can do all sorts of harmful things—harmful to others, but also harmful to themselves. When you recognize that their crazy emotions are making them act in this way, you view them differently. Looking at the situation broadly, you can see that such behavior is not in the person's interest. You can reflect that in his or her saner moments, the person would never have acted that way.

Another option is to envision their action as the result of a poison or drug that they themselves have taken unknowingly. In fact, you can reflect that had they not been overpowered or drugged by afflictive emotions, they would never have engaged in that harmful behavior. When you recognize that they are victims of their own emotions, you make space for sympathy and affection for them to grow. Any love you felt for them before they harmed you can be reawakened. Ultimately, your yearning to see other people free of the suffering they are creating for themselves can outweigh your concern about what they are doing to you.

Shifting your concern from your own well-being to include a genuine concern for the other person can transform your relationships, and it can also transform you as a person. You can become a person who provides well-being to others, and who shoulders the burden for others, too. This is a very uncomplicated shift in outlook that can completely reorient your relationships. I think this outlook might yield the healthiest relationships of all.

4 ◆ Gender Identities
It's All in the Mind

ALTHOUGH WE HAVE LIMITLESS POTENTIAL, we can end up feeling boxed in to a particular role in life or a particular understanding of who we are. How does this happen? We limit ourselves when we adopt specific identities, and then believe that this is truly who we are and must be. We can see this clearly happening with gender.

Often gender seems to define our place in the world and our life experiences, even though it is nothing more than a socially constructed identity. Our ideas about what it means to be a woman or a man—that is, our gender constructs—are given meaning and importance in our day-to-day reality. Gender identities permeate so much of our experience that is it easy to forget that they are just ideas—ideas created to categorize human beings. Nevertheless, the categories of masculine and feminine are often treated as if they were eternal truths. But they are not. They have no objective reality. Because gender is a concept, it is a product of our mind—and has no absolute existence that is separate from the mind that conceives of it. Gender categories are not inherently real in and of themselves.

Nevertheless, our gender shapes our experiences when it comes to form part of our sense of self—or what I discussed as our "fabricated I" in chapter 3, "Healthy Relationships." We construct and hold on to certain identities for women and different identities for men. In other words, there are fabricated masculine "I"s and fabricated feminine "I"s—and they are all just ideas we have created.

Social "Realities"

Though they have no objective reality, gender constructs affect our place in society. They influence how much pay we receive for the jobs we do, and the roles we play at home in the family. They affect which aspects of our personalities we feel comfortable expressing and which we do not. They can determine the clothes we wear, and they can impact our relationship to our own body.

Societies take the distinction between masculine and feminine qualities very seriously indeed. Whole industries reinforce gender ideals, such as, for example, boys should be brave and girls should be sensitive. Society promotes the idea that people with Y chromosomes should exhibit only "masculine qualities," and people with X chromosomes should exhibit "feminine qualities." This holds us back, limiting men and women to socially constructed boxes, and causing a great deal of suffering for everyone.

In my own personal case, I do not always feel clear about this distinction between masculine and feminine qualities. People have told me that I have more feminine qualities than masculine. I do not know quite what that means. I just have a sense of what these qualities feel like, but I have no labels of "feminine" or "masculine" to go with the feelings. I simply experience them.

For me personally, knowing how to define and categorize such things is not important. What matters to me is being able to connect with others heart to heart, with real feeling. What I value is the ability to speak from my heart, and to be tender and caring. I hope I have some of these qualities. Certainly these are the qualities I aspire to have. It does not strike me as at all relevant whether they are categorized as feminine or masculine.

Balance Requires Both

No matter how we divide up the complete set of positive human qualities, I believe that whether we are men or women, each of us needs to develop all positive qualities—those society calls masculine, and those it calls feminine. This is an idea taught within Tibetan Buddhism. In Tibetan Buddhist texts, wisdom and skillful means are two highly valued spiritual qualities: wisdom is conceptualized as a feminine quality; skillful means—the quality of being adept at finding ways to accomplish one's objectives—is conceptualized as masculine. The best possible result comes when the two are joined, and therefore these "masculine" and "feminine" qualities should be integrated in every person.

Tibetan Buddhism is well-known for its depictions of deities in sexual union. These symbolize the integration of masculine and feminine qualities. Many Westerners jump to the wrong conclusion that these images have something to do with the *Kama Sutra,* and are maybe something vaguely Hindu, but are certainly something biological and connected with sex. This is a complete misunderstanding. Rather, these images remind us that—however a given society may label different personal traits—everyone needs both those considered feminine and those considered masculine. Tibetan texts teach that the highest spiritual awakening that a human being is capable of cannot be achieved without the union of wisdom and skillful means. In other words, we cannot become a buddha unless both the qualities that are labeled "feminine" and the qualities labeled "masculine" are present and integrated within us. This reminds us that we all have within us the capacity to develop every positive quality. More than that, it shows us that it is beneficial and important for us to have all these positive qualities, regardless of the gender they are associated with.

For that reason, instead of feeling uncomfortable about having both feminine and masculine traits, I think we should feel unbalanced if we have only one or the other! We should feel most comfortable when we have both sets of qualities within us.

In Asia there is the idea of yin, a feminine principle, and yang, a masculine one. Native American traditions speak of Mother Earth and Father Sky. We need both together to have a whole world. Since we need both aspects to be balanced and whole people as well, it is absurd that people are subject to ridicule for having both masculine and feminine qualities. In any case, the definition of masculine and feminine qualities differs from one culture to another. None of these gender constructs are permanent. Just like the rest of our fabricated identities, gender identities are fluid.

Evolving with the Times

Because gender ideals are fluid and not fixed, they change with the times. The definitions of gender roles in particular societies are based on what is suited to the given time or place. We can see this in prehistoric times, when human beings had to fight and hunt to ensure the survival of the clan or species. For such purposes, physical force and aggressiveness were valued. Due to men's superior physical strength, they took on a more important role during this era when society depended on brute force. But times have changed. Society's needs have changed. We no longer need to divide ourselves into hunters and gatherers. We now need to work together to produce peace, harmony, a compassionate outlook, and loving care.

In this era of global communication and weapons of mass destruction, rather than impose our will on others by force, we urgently need to find ways to accommodate divergent wills. It has been a long and gradual process, but I believe the world is slowly coming to realize that what we need now is not the ability to make assertions, but the ability to listen. Especially with the unthinkably destructive power of the weapons we have at our disposal, it seems clear that we need to sit down to dialogue, and not stand up to fight.

The times call on us to look at others with the attentive and loving eyes of a mother, rather than with the hostile eyes of a warrior in battle. If we are going to divide up qualities as masculine or feminine, I think we have to say that the qualities we need today are qualities more often described as feminine. We need communication and sensitive listening to others' needs—qualities that are likelier to be identified as feminine than masculine in most societies.

It is time we truly recognize that the era of the hunter is past. This should be a more "feminine" era—an era when women make greater contributions to society. If we continue to devalue what women have to offer, we will continue harming women and continue overlooking and devaluing these virtues that are considered "feminine." And these are precisely the virtues that the world needs most now.

Women's Rights Are Human Rights

For this reason, I believe it is imperative that we change our basic ideas about gender and women's rights. I have to admit something: when I was first exposed to the notion of "rights," it didn't move me. This might have been because the word used in Tibetan to translate the concept of "rights" includes the word for "gaining" or "winning," and can also mean "portion." The discussion left me with the impression that we were fighting over who gets a share of limited goods, as if one person's right to gain something meant other people had to lose. So fighting for rights sounded like seeking to defeat others and take something away from them—like some kind of zero-sum game. When you think of rights in that way, it sounds as if women's rights must involve taking something away from men.

Much later, I participated in a TED conference in India. (TED is a nonprofit organization devoted to "Ideas Worth Sharing.") Hearing how people spoke about rights at that conference opened a new way of thinking for me. I learned something especially important from a conversation I had with a feminist activist during that conference. She led me to change my earlier understanding about women's rights. There was no translator present when we met, and I did not understand everything she said. But she spoke very emphatically, with great feeling for the issue. As she was talking, I recognized that this was a matter of basic human rights. It became clear to me that women's rights are nothing other than human rights. Those who work for women's rights are seeking to secure for women what all human beings need and deserve.

The Particular Sufferings of Women

I would like to share something personal with you. I think of myself as a person who has a healthy relationship with his parents. In spite of that, I escaped from Tibet and consequently left them behind. I felt that the reasons to go outweighed the reasons to stay, so I made that sacrifice. It still remains to be seen whether I will be able to fully accomplish the goals for which I left my home behind, and which made it seem worth leaving at the time. I retain a deep love for my parents, and my love is especially deep toward my mother. But I do not know whether I will see her again.

I actively try to heighten my awareness of the particular sufferings of women. Based on the love I feel for my own mother in this life, my approach is to see all women in the world as my mother, and seek to benefit them. There are certain kinds of suffering that women face just because they are women. It is my resolve and aspiration to dedicate my whole life to ending the suffering of others. Whatever the result of my efforts may be, I wish to dedicate my life to easing their pain and changing the difficult circumstances that women face.

Even with all the social progress we have had, it seems that in many parts of the world, women are still not fully treated as human beings. The violence committed against women suggests they are seen not as people, but as objects. Although gender constructs are mere concepts, we can see that they can be terribly powerful forces that shape our experiences and affect how we treat others. When we hold on to socially constructed gender categories, thinking they reflect actual reality, we can fail to see the individual human being, fixating instead on the labels we have stuck to them.

I have seen reports suggesting that in India a woman is raped every three minutes. The figures are similar for the United States. This is a very, very serious situation. These statistics make it clear that seeking women's rights has nothing to do with winning or losing, or taking anything away from men. Women's rights have to do with respecting the value of human life and freedom. It has to do with acknowledging our shared humanity and the basic human bonds that link us.

This respectful awareness is not something that can be legislated or created by economic strategies. The very fact that rape is still so common although it is against the law shows that legislation alone is not enough. When we talk about legal rights, we must consider who controls and enforces the laws, and how laws can be manipulated by different parties. The same holds true for creating economic opportunities for women. These measures need to be in place, but they are not nearly enough. The problem goes beyond legislation or social policy. The solution must be rooted much more deeply within us, and the change has to take place at a much deeper level—the level of our attitudes.

Effecting change in women's rights is not like moving an object out of harm's reach. As long as the harmful attitudes remain, women's well-being will continue to be in danger. External change cannot take place without inner change. When a problem is rooted in a society's habitual outlook and habitual thinking, then legislating change will have limited effect. After all, you cannot legislate a change in thinking.

We Tibetan Buddhists have an opportunity to do something

practical to improve matters by instating full monastic ordination for women. Full ordination was available for women in India, but was never fully established in Tibet. Initially, I thought that the main obstacle to doing so lay in the monastic rules and policies. But I later realized that the real problem was society's thinking about nuns and about women. Now I feel that we will only be able to accomplish our goal when Tibetan society comes to see how valuable it would be to have fully ordained women.

I think a note of caution is in order here. Although there may be aspects of Buddhist teachings that can help us in thinking more wisely about gender issues, I want to warn you against looking to Buddhist societies to provide ideal examples of healthy gender constructs and practices. You should expect to come across things you do not want to adopt for yourself. Not everything in Buddhist institutions is perfect, and this is certainly the case when it comes to gender discrimination.

Gender Ideals Hurt Men, Too

As important as it is to address the impact of gender constructs on the lives of women, we should also keep in mind that fabricated gender identities are problematic for men as well as women. Men are bound by social roles, just as women are. Society's habitual views of gender are imposed upon us all.

In Tibet, too, problems with gender constructs affect both men and women. For example, in many cultures crying is considered "unmanly." In Kham, the region where I was born, men are expected to be "brave." This was the trait Khampa men were traditionally supposed to display, and it is still encouraged today. In ancient times, it was a sign of great valor for a Khampa to die in a war; that was the sign of being a "real man." To be a "real man," you took revenge on others through violent means. Men were told not to have fear when they were attacked. In fact, a "manly man" would invite his opponent to land the first blow. Then, when his opponent hit him, he was not supposed to cry out or show any pain. There even used to be a practice that if a man wanted to show how brave he was, he fought naked with just his sword. You have never seen anything like the way they fought with swords in that part of Tibet. There was no technique, no kung fu, no finesse. They would just slug it out with swords. If this were made into an action adventure film, it might do very well in Hollywood!

As for myself, I am a Khampa, but I do not like to take an aggressive stance or oppose others at all. People who watch out for my interests sometimes advise me to be less earnest and to go on the offensive more. They caution me against being so open and trusting. They warn me that people can have all sorts of different motivations and ulterior motives, and may be out to deceive me or use my name for their own ends. Even though I have heard this advice clearly, I cannot change. Actually, I don't want to.

The Biological Basis

Unlike gender identities, which are social constructs, we know that there are some real biological differences between men and women. This is obvious. If the aim is to become completely identical—to erase any distinction whatsoever between men and women—that is not really an option, because there are certain physical distinctions that cannot be denied. Of course, some people may want to change that biological distinction medically, too, and that is fine, but generally the biological difference is there.

But what we can change is what these biological differences mean socially. The social meaning of our biological differences is created by our ideas about gender—that is, what gender means socially is determined by the mind, and not by the body. "Masculine" and "feminine" are fabricated identities that societies create, not nature. When we think in more subtle ways beyond obvious anatomical distinctions, we see that the fundamental foundation of human beings includes both female and male aspects, both psychologically and even biologically. We have both.

In the Judeo-Christian tradition, the dominant view is that first there was man, and woman came later. But in Buddhist texts, a very different story is told. There is a Buddhist account that asserts that in the beginning, there was no gender or sex at all. There were no men or women, just human beings. Everyone was equal, socially and biologically.

However, as these human beings consumed more and more of the earth's natural resources, they became increasingly arrogant. At a certain point, according to this account, they began eating a special plant that produced new fruit almost as soon as its old fruit was plucked. Eating the fruit caused humans to develop distinct organs, and thus the species divided into men and women. It was not just women who ate the fruit, but all human beings—those who became men as well as those who became women.

This story imagines that there was a time when you could be human without being either a man or a woman. This suggests that being human is prior to being male or female.

As I understand it, Western medicine teaches that biologically we all start out female. During the formation of the fetus in the womb, initially human beings are female, and only later do some human beings transform from female to male. This is also the understanding in Tibetan medical texts, which explain that the difference between men and women depends on whether the sexual organ has become manifest or remains internal.

Basically, if you want to divide society into categories based on physical differences, you can find a basis for doing so. But there is no requirement that we make such divisions. And the way we construct identities around these divisions is quite arbitrary. In other words, as I have been saying, gender constructs are nothing more than social fabrications. It is only social conditions and our own concepts that make gender constructs seem real and absolute.

Harmful Images of the Body

In general, I believe we have gotten ourselves into a great deal of trouble by exaggerating the importance of the body. Many people seem to believe that happiness can come from the body. This is an absurd expectation. It reveals a serious confusion between transitory sense gratification and full and stable happiness. This confusion has led us to have deeply unhealthy relationships with our own body.

Gender ideals tend to give our body an exaggerated role in our life and our identity. This is another example of confusion, and of mistaking a fabricated identity for who we really are. Gender constructs include images of what a male or female body should ideally look like. As absurd as this notion is, many people actually begin to feel that their personal identity and happiness are dependent on how closely their body fits that ideal. If we are looking to our body as a source of happiness—or to tell us something meaningful about who we are—we have already entered into a completely unrealistic relationship with our own body.

Unhealthy relationships to our body manifest in various ways. Some people undergo cosmetic surgery, trying to hide the natural and inevitable signs of aging. Others develop eating disorders. Some people eat too much, looking for their own pleasure, while others force themselves to undereat in an attempt to attract others.

Some people think that having a thin body can bring them happiness. But when they lose weight and do not automatically become happy, rather than realize that this is not where happiness comes from, they think instead that the problem is that they are not skinny enough. Anorexia is a terrible sickness that amounts to self-imposed starvation. I saw a news report about an anorexic model in France who died because she literally starved herself to death. Frankly, she was so thin she looked less like a human being than a walking skeleton. This is terribly sad, and completely pointless.

Some people spend many hours in the gym trying to get their body to look a certain way. As in the case of excessive dieting, such activity can also be motivated by a wish to have their body match a mental ideal of what they should look like, and those ideals are very much based on gender constructs, too.

Please do not let gender constructs trick you into thinking that having a certain kind of body can bring you happiness and remove suffering. This is entirely mistaken. Happiness is not defined by body shape or size. It is not defined by skin color, either.

This seems so obvious that it should go without saying, but when we look around us, we can see that this message still has not sunk in. In India, there are products that people use to lighten their skin. I have heard that in the West, some people lie in the sun to make their skin darker. These are absurd attempts to use our body to make us feel happy with ourselves. When these attempts at happiness fail, we should use our mind to analyze where the problem really lies. And we really ought to ask ourselves how we as a society have come to the point of actually believing in the idea that our happiness depends on the shape and color of our body.

Find Your Value Within

It does not matter how close your body comes to what society says is ideal for your gender. No amount of physical "perfection" can bring lasting happiness or sustain you through life's ups and downs. What can sustain you are your own virtuous thoughts and noble heart. No matter how things look on the outside, when you have goodness inside you, you will always have something in your heart that you can treasure. If you feel that you have reasons to dislike yourself because of your body or because of ideas about gender, just look within to the virtuous thoughts you have had, and you will always find a reason to love yourself. Take joy in your sincere intentions. Everything starts with an intention.

If you have been able to have beautiful aspirations, these aspirations will always be part of you, a beautiful part.

The deepest reasons to love yourself have nothing to do with anything outside you—not with your body or with others' expectations of you. If you ground yourself in your own goodness, nothing will be able to damage your self-esteem. Take delight in your inner nature, in your virtues, in all your beautiful qualities, regardless of whether they are labeled masculine or feminine. It starts that way.

As long as you stay connected with the goodness deep within you, your love for yourself will be firm enough to withstand any challenge from gender conceptions that were not realistic to begin with.

Dropping Unrealistic Expectations

It is important to base your sense of your own worth in your own inner goodness, for several reasons. First, so you do not start looking to outer things to define you, but also because if you internalize gender ideals, these can work on you negatively from within. Gender constructs are ideas, and therefore they influence our thinking. They create expectations, and can also result in a negative self-image when you take those expectations too seriously. If your self-esteem is low and your ideals are high, then the gap between the two can seem hopelessly unbridgeable.

This is something I know about from experience. The Karmapa is supposed to perform the enlightened activities of the buddhas—talk about high standards! For my own part, I feel that I'm an ordinary person who is often the victim of my own habitual tendencies. As the Karmapa, I need to be someone who others look up to. I am not supposed to have even one single fault, yet of course I have innumerable faults. There is such a huge gap between these expectations and how I see myself, and as a result, I do not always feel that good about myself. Though

I can honestly say that I mean well, I cannot accomplish everything I wish to.

The discrepancy between what we need to do or want to do, and what we actually can do, could easily become a reason to feel bad about ourselves. In this way, we are all in a similar situation. What is helpful is to drop your expectations about yourself.

Do not let anyone tell you how you must look or act just because you are a man or a woman. You have boundless potential that can only be limited when you believe that your social identity is really who you are. Who you are is not a perfectly measured object. There is tremendous elasticity in who you can be. It is up to you to decide the shape you give yourself.

5 ✦ Consumerism and Greed
Contentment Is the Best Wealth

WE HAVE BEEN LOOKING AT how we come to be limited by the identities we adopt. How we interact with the world also shapes us—and it shapes the world itself, too. The way we commonly relate to material objects has resulted in a culture of consumerism. But we have the potential to relate to things differently, and therefore to modify our shared culture, as well as our own personal relationship to our belongings.

Everything we own is ultimately made of material extracted from the earth and the sea. These natural resources all have limits, but the greed that drives our consumption of those resources has no limit built in to it. It is up to us to actively limit our own greed. We often fail to do so, in part because we believe that greed is simply natural. This is an assumption I would like to call into question. I believe I can demonstrate that we can rid ourselves of greed, because it is not an innate part of us. Doing so will allow us to cultivate a healthier personal relationship to the material goods we own. It can also yield a healthier society, less focused on acquisition and less inclined to confuse happiness with material wealth.

If we look at the condition of our planet, I think we can agree that there is an urgent need to change our generation's patterns of consumption. Our current exploitation of the earth's resources exceeds all natural bounds, driven as it is by an unlimited quest for more. If we continue like this, the time will definitely come when our means of sustaining ourselves reaches its natural limit.

It seems as if our century's contribution to world history will be to consume natural resources at unprecedented rates. Scientists tell us that we have consumed one-third of the planet's resources in the past thirty years alone. At this rate, we will have turned our planet into a barren rock well before the twenty-first century is over.

When that happens, clearly our very survival on this planet will be endangered. Even if it takes longer than these figures suggest, our pace of consumption is leading rapidly toward the depletion of the earth's resources. We may not feel particularly concerned about our own survival, but the earth does not belong to us alone. We share this planet with future generations. No matter how challenging it may be, we are responsible for changing our patterns of consumption so that human life on this earth is sustainable, now and in the centuries to come.

We each have this responsibility, because we are all participants in consumption. In the name of progress or social status, we feel we need new electronics, a new car, or a new house. Then we are obliged to buy even more things in order to outfit and maintain what we have just acquired. All of these goods have to come from somewhere. And all of the things we are replacing when we "upgrade" have to be put somewhere. We tend to focus on the goods we are currently using, and on the immediate gratification we get from them. We rarely look beyond that to the impact of our consumption—its short-term and long-term consequences. These consequences should be immediately obvious to us, but they aren't, not at all. When we do take a longer view, we can see very clearly that this kind of consumption cannot be sustained for much longer. Things simply have to change.

We Can Be Agents of Change

One effect of globalization is that more and more of the people on this planet are being encouraged to join in the culture of consumption, which until now only some countries' economies have been able to support. So-called developed countries have been setting the pace that other countries now seek to match. As more and more people join in the race to acquire and consume, we will all be moving even faster toward the depletion of our planet's resources. This places an added responsibility on developed countries to think deeply about the trends they are setting for others.

But who will take up the responsibility to bring about change? We might naturally turn to our government to take the lead in a public matter of such widely shared concern. Many people do expect that governments will be the agents of this change. After all, they are supposed to play the central role in looking after their people's well-being and the country's future.

However, for the most part, those governments that could take up such a challenge do so very selectively. They might take steps to protect some of their own natural resources, yet freely allow the import of those same resources from elsewhere, without inquiring into how they were extracted. They might clean up their own houses, but do so by dumping their waste and problems in another country. Initially, this hurts people in those other countries who have to live with the garbage dumped there, but eventually it also harms those who dumped the trash in the first place. The world has become a large family, sharing one large house. Tossing our garbage in one corner of the house still leaves us all with a dirty house. Damaging the beams of one room makes the whole structure unstable.

If we cannot count on the world's governments to make positive change, we might think of turning to large corporations, since multinational corporations are largely setting the course of development throughout the world. Yet here too, we know what we are up against. The primary aim of such corporations is to generate profit, not to generate peace and happiness for all.

As we see, we cannot shift the responsibility to others. For one thing, it is clear that this just will not work. For another, we bear a responsibility. Who are the large corporations producing goods for? For us consumers. We are a key part of the problem. We hold far more power than we usually think. We individuals can become part of the solution when we recognize this power and start to use it, together.

One Planet, Many Heroes

We do not have to wait for others to make the right choices. We ourselves can join together and collectively begin to make sound choices about our consumption, and thus find the right way forward. If we want the system to change, we consumers must give a definite, consistent signal to governments and corporations that together we are determined to change our behavior and our attitudes. We are the ones choosing what to buy, and also whether to even buy at all. We can communicate our commitment to the issue by only buying certain products, and we can exercise our option not to buy at all.

The amount of work that needs to be undertaken is great, and we bear an enormous responsibility. The future of the world really does depend on this. We cannot wait for others to act. Who is the hero who can save the world? It is you. It is every one of us. If you accept this challenge, that would be truly heroic. You would be an altruistic hero.

Expecting one hero to save the world is not going to work like it does in the movies. If everything depended on one person, then when that one person was killed, or just got tired, it would be all over for the world. In any case, we do not need to wait for someone else to step in and lead us. Every one of us already has access to the tools we need in order to put change in motion. And we all need to use those tools together, because this job is too big for any one hero. When I first escaped from Tibet and came to India, a magazine named me an "Asian Hero of the Year." But they did not name me alone; they name several "heroes" each year. They understand that Asia and the world need many heroes. We need as many heroes as the task demands.

To be true heroes, we need to generate a noble aspiration. We resolve with all our heart to work to benefit others, no matter what. A truly noble resolve can produce noble conduct. Those who harbor noble aspirations for the world and engage in noble conduct are what we call "bodhisattvas." In Tibetan, we refer to such bodhisattvas as heroes, for it is noble aspiration and noble conduct that make a person a hero. Any one of us can ground our actions in our nobility of heart, and become heroes.

Changing Course

We can all become heroes in pioneering a new course that leads away from a global culture based mainly on buying and selling more stuff. The first step is to educate ourselves so we understand clearly why we need to change course, as well as how to do so.

To answer the call to change our habitual culture of consumption, we need to understand the role and nature of greed. We each need to get clear for ourselves just how destructive greed is. Greed and the consumerism it leads to cause serious harm—to us on a personal level, to our society, and to the planet. As we have seen, greed has devastating effects on the natural environment. It blinds us to the global impact of our craving for acquisition. It also poses a real obstacle to our personal happiness. Our greed keeps us focused on what we do not yet have, and blinds us to all that we already have. Greed guarantees that no matter how much we acquire, it will never, ever be enough. Building a society or a life based on greed is a recipe for dissatisfaction, plain and simple.

One obstacle that has kept our societies from seriously tackling the problem of greed is a nagging suspicion that it can never be eliminated. Deep down, we may feel that it is just part of human nature. But greed is not inherent to our nature. It arises because certain causes and conditions come together. If greed were a natural and integral part of a person, it would be constantly present, under all conditions, yet we can see that it is there at some times and not others. How could greed come and go in us if it were naturally present all the time as part of us? Why would some people exhibit so much more of it than other people if all human beings were naturally greedy?

There is no need to take my word for this. We have many opportunities to see how greed comes and goes within us. We can actually watch it develop gradually in our own mind out of an attitude of clinging or grasping. Advertising and commercials are highly effective mechanisms for generating greed. Within Asia, India is famous for its TV commercials. I have seen a commercial with Jackie Chan and Buddhist monks flying off together into the sky, riding the latest motorcycle model. When we first see such commercials, they are so ridiculous that they are funny. At first, they just make us laugh. But in the end, we really want that motorcycle!

How does this happen? We all want to be happy, but generally we lack a clear idea of where real happiness comes from. The commercials communicate certain ideas about what we need in order to feel happy. When we are repeatedly exposed to these images and ideas, they begin to form a kind of mental habit. We start feeling that what was advertised could be the key to our happiness, and so of course we want to own it. We end up telling ourselves, "I should have one of those motorcycles! I should go around in style! I want to be successful and happy, too!"

Over time, we develop a habit of longing for what we do not have. Without our noticing where it came from, this habitual desire creeps up on us and evolves into greed. Like other habits, greed develops gradually. We do not stop to check this growing habit in its early stages, because for the most part our cultures encourage us to give ourselves over to greed. The more deeply ingrained our habit of greed, the more deeply we fall under its sway—and the more "natural" it seems. Once entrenched, the habit of greed keeps us feeling needy, and forever on the lookout for things we lack. In short, greed makes us unhappy.

I want to underscore this point: we find greed difficult to control not because it is natural, but because it has been generated by long, unchecked habituation. This is important to recognize, because even though old habits may be tough to break, all habits can be broken.

Human Gullibility and the Allure of Goods

I find two factors presented in Buddhist texts to be very useful in understanding how greed is produced within us. One factor is what is described as the "fickle and deceptive display of phenomena." This refers to the fact that things themselves can appear in an endless number of ways that are misleading, and have nothing whatsoever to do with reality. The other factor is our gullible mind. When these two conditions come together, it is dangerous. We are easily tricked, as our gullibility leads us to believe those misleading appearances.

To see how this works, we can look again at consumer marketing. This industry brings to bear the full force of human ingenuity in exploiting these two factors—our gullibility and the deceptiveness of appearances. The result is the most alluring display of consumer goods possible.

In the past, there were great meditators who saw the futility of pursuing sense pleasures, which of course includes consumer goods. They lived in true renunciation and were entirely free of desire and greed. Sometimes I joke that even those meditators might have been in trouble if they had lived in the twenty-first century, given how sophisticated the marketing experts have become in manipulating how things appear. If someone were to offer them a smartphone, their steely resolve might be able to weather it. But then someone might give them an iPad. For a while they might be fine, until they heard about the next version, with all the great new features. Then they might really be in trouble!

Products are specially designed to catch the eye and captivate the mind. Because we focus on what else there is to acquire, rather than what we already have, we fall into the endless upgrade game. "The functions you need are coming in the next version! The new design is so much more attractive! And it comes in your favorite color!" These products may be mass-produced, but they are custom-made to suit our greed and grasping. They are exactly tailored to deceive us with their appearances.

As I see it, however, the bigger problem is the gullibility of our mind. This is what really leaves us vulnerable to the deceptive allure of things. In other words, we ourselves are the bigger problem. Sometimes we are like small children; when it comes to assessing our own needs, we often show no sign of maturity. Just think about it: When a little child cries, the easy way to stop him is to give him a toy. We dangle it in front of him and wave it around to catch his attention until he reaches out to grab it. When we finally hand over the toy, he quiets down. Our goal was just to stop his crying. We did not try to address the child's underlying needs. We gave him something else to desire, and tricked him into falling silent for the time being.

As adults, we also use our electronics and other consumer "toys" for a similar purpose—to distract ourselves from whatever is really troubling us. But in our case, we say it is just for a little fun, a little entertainment. Our consumption is often limited to such short-term ends, with no concern for the long-term habits we are developing, or the wider impact of our actions. We seldom even ask ourselves why we felt dissatisfied or needy in the first place.

We need to realize that there is something terribly wrong with letting our craving and greed drive us to consume in this way. We are being blinded by our greed, and it is up to us to open our own eyes. It is up to us to act. Greed has no limits of its own. It is something we ourselves must recognize, counteract, and actively limit.

I do want to acknowledge that there are many forces surrounding us that encourage us to follow along unthinkingly wherever our greed leads us. We are bombarded by advertising designed to convince us that our happiness depends on material goods. Today's global culture tells us that having more of these goods is a measure of our success in life, and even of our value as a person. This message comes at us in many forms and from many directions, so we need a clear awareness of how greed works in order to protect ourselves from being deceived by these forces. We can then counteract them with inner wisdom about where real success and personal value come from. In this way, even if we cannot eliminate the basic deceptiveness of appearances—or the social and commercial forces seeking to exploit them—we can certainly reduce our own gullibility to them.

Making It Personal

In the face of these outer forces, our efforts to change our patterns of consumption are truly admirable and even heroic. To stay on course in those efforts, it is extremely useful to connect what we understand about greed directly to our own experiences. Some people may wonder, "Is it really so bad to want things?" In my view, the main problem is that we believe that getting everything we want will make us happy. This leads us to feel that we need all those things in order to be happy. For all our intelligence and sophistication, we end up acting as if money will literally buy us happiness. This attitude underlies our consumerist lifestyles and societies.

Using our own personal experience, we can ask ourselves where the distinction lies between what we really need in order to be happy, and what we do not need but merely want. Greed takes control of us when we lose sight of this distinction and mistake our wants for needs.

For example, you decide to go shopping for a watch. You enter the store and are shown one watch after another, each with more features and a nicer design than the last. What you need is a way to tell time. But what you soon want are the fanciest and most expensive watches. You want those bells and whistles that have nothing to do with the time of day. The watches are all so nice, you soon reach the point where you have a craving to buy many watches.

Greed is ridiculous, making us grab at things like babies grasping for a rattle! When you find yourself pining greedily after things in this way, you can stop for a moment and conduct the following thought experiment. First, step back and look carefully at your actual needs. Ask yourself whether the object is something you really need, or just something you want. In the case of the watch, you might say to yourself, "Do I really need another watch?" You can be playful and ask yourself, "What am I going to do with more than one watch? Can I wear a watch on each hand, and another two on my feet? Do I need watches on my ankles so that the insects walking past me can also tell the time?" Your conclusion then might be: "I want many watches, but I do not need more than one watch." The idea here is to make the distinction between an actual need and a mere desire as clear for yourself as you can.

If you determine that you actually do need to buy the object, then your next step is to assess what real function it needs to perform for you. That assessment can then guide your particular purchase. In the case of a watch, you can reflect that you need it to tell the time of day, and it should fit your wrist comfortably. These are your practical, physical necessities. Anything beyond that is just your consumer mind running crazy.

These two steps might help you keep yourself sane! Otherwise, if you let the craziness of greed control you, even something as simple as buying a watch can become an agonizing experience.

I think we could all benefit from taking a closer look at how ridiculously we act when greed has us in its grip. In Tibet, we applied a very specific criterion in choosing goods. We looked for something durable. Our definition of a good item was something that would fulfill a function and last a long time—not how impressive it looked. When we Tibetans arrived in exile, our thoughts turned to appearances, and all of our concerns for the durability of goods disappeared. We were overtaken by greed, and became its puppets. This was a serious case of greed—we were driven by greed to chase after our wants, rather than living with contentment when our needs were met.

Once we have decided that we do not wish to continue living as greed's puppets, we have the option of grounding ourselves in a clear assessment of what we need. We do not have to let our desires control us. In the task of challenging our own greed, our basic intelligence and honest introspection are powerful allies. When we apply them, we can identify when our greed is telling us we "need" something that we actually do not.

It is important that we develop the habit of distinguishing between wants and needs, because much more than just our own personal well-being is at stake. We only have to look at the rapid degradation of our natural environment in order to see the destructive effects of our consumerism. When we see polluted streams and smoggy valleys and deforested hillsides, we are looking at the results of our unchecked consumerism. With eyes open, we can clearly see the predicament we have created for ourselves and for the world. This situation we are in was caused by shortsightedness and a profound ignorance. It comes from our failure to see the interdependence between our collective actions and the world we share. Therefore, the problem can be solved by taking a long view, and by judiciously applying our wisdom in order to understand the reality of that interdependence.

Buying as Connecting

Awareness of interdependence helps to counteract greed, because greed only arises when we treat ourselves as fundamentally independent and disconnected from others. With greed, we see ourselves as not only separate from other people, but even in competition with them. The most important words in greed's vocabulary are "my" and "mine." If we look at what underlies greed, we can find a fundamentally self-centered fixation on our own interests.

To the degree that greed controls us, we are basically living inside a cage created by our own selfishness. It is like when a person is placed in jail. Only a few visitors can gain entry—a few family members or close friends—and the prisoner is otherwise cut off from the outside world. In a similar way, our self-centeredness also locks us away in a sort of prison. It lets in just those few people that we recognize as important to our well-being—"my" family or "my" friends. Then it keeps everyone else at a distance. It leaves us feeling disconnected, cut off, and alone. Our self-absorption severely impedes our awareness of others. It hampers a sense of closeness to other people, and blinds us to the ties of interdependence that always connect us to one another.

When we are trapped in this prison of our own self-fixation, we feel and act as if the rest of the world doesn't exist. But it does exist. Even prisoners in solitary isolation live in dependence on the outside world. We all depend on others, and thereby are connected to others at all times. This is an indisputable fact of our basic existence on this planet. It is painful to live unaware of those connections. We are only blinded to them by our habitual self-centeredness, and we can open our eyes to them by consciously training ourselves to look beyond our immediate concerns and see the wider view.

The truth of interdependence can be observed in every single act of consumption. Simple analysis reveals that nothing we buy is an independent object. Every consumer good on the market is made up of discrete parts. When a product arrives in our hands, it may appear to be a complete and single entity, but it was constructed from multiple substances or smaller parts.

I would like to suggest a simple exercise to help us free ourselves from the habitual self-centeredness that underlies greed. This exercise uses consumer goods to awaken us to our interdependence and connectedness to others.

You can use anything, but let's take a backpack as the example for this exercise. It could be the backpack that you carry this book in. Take the backpack in your hands, and really look at it for a moment.

Reflect on the various materials that it is made of. All these different materials have probably been assembled from different corners of the world. Some parts come from somewhere to the east, others from the west, and still others from off to the south. Its apparent wholeness is the result of numerous contributions from many different quarters.

The fabric, the thread, the dyes, the design, the company that ordered it made, the factory—all of these play an integral part in the creation of that one backpack. Many preceding steps—thousands of steps—went into the making of every single object we acquire. And all of these steps involve numerous people.

As your next step in this exercise, take a moment to acknowledge all the people who were involved in producing this single backpack and also in delivering it into your hands right now—the designers, the factory workers, the shippers, the truck drivers, the shop owner, the salespeople, the clerks, the cashier—many people's efforts joined together to bring it within your reach. See if you can recognize their presence there with you in the object you hold in your hands. You can carry this one backpack around thanks to all of them—thanks to countless other beings.

As a final step, with an awareness of this relationship to others, you can mentally reach out to them in gratitude. Through this backpack, you are now closely connected to them by the fact that you are using the results of their efforts, and quite possibly their suffering. In other words, you are connected to them in happiness and suffering. You can resolve to carry the backpack with an awareness of the responsibility that this relationship implies.

I think reflecting in this way could allow you to use your belongings to recognize your connectedness to others, rather than letting them block others from your view. It could also help you establish a healthier relationship to the material objects you own.

You can bring this perspective of interdependence to bear when you are acquiring new goods as well. When you consider purchasing something, you should not only think about whether you can afford it. You should think about the cost to the planet and about the labor of those who produced it for you. You can also think that this product is available for you to purchase because of the efforts of many others. You are dependent on them for your happiness, and they are dependent on you.

I think it would be very powerful to take each act of acquisition as a reminder of our interdependence. Every single purchase can signal to us—if we let it—all that we are receiving from the many people involved in producing it. This awareness of our interdependence should be a cause for our love and affectionate regard for others to increase. It can keep us aware of the impact our consumption has on others and on the planet. If we connect to others and to the planet with love and affection, our responsibility to bring about change does not have to weigh heavily on us at all. We will carry it gladly.

Money and Happiness

As we scrutinize our relationship to our own belongings, it might be worth asking ourselves some basic questions. What are we looking for from the things we own? Do we seek to accumulate objects of enjoyment, hoping to gain happiness from them? Or have we lost sight of the aim of happiness, and just given ourselves over to the accumulation of stuff? Are we looking primarily to be "well-off," or to be happy?

I would like to tell you a story that addresses these questions. This tale takes place long, long ago, in a faraway land where there lived a very wealthy man. In the street next to this man's mansion, there lived a beggar in a simple little shack. The beggar ate what little he could beg by day, and came home each night with nothing, while right next door, the owner of the mansion brought home bags of money every day. The rich man spent his evenings at home counting his money, while the beggar spent his evenings in his rundown shack singing.

Every night, the rich man heard the poor man singing, and one day he thought, "This makes no sense. What does he have to enjoy in life? He has nothing, but he's always singing. How could he be so happy?"

The wealthy man decided to investigate. One day, when the poor man had gone out to beg, the wealthy man placed a huge bar of gold in his shack. When the poor man returned and saw the gold, he thought, "Someone must have lost this, so I should find out who, and return it to them." But then he had a second thought: "Maybe it was left here on purpose. I bet some rich person felt sorry for me and left it here on purpose."

This idea began to take possession of his mind. He started thinking of the gold as his, and began laying plans how to spend it. First, he'd sell the bar of gold. Then he'd build a house and start a family, and go on vacations to distant places. But somehow he would also need to save enough money to pay for everything his children would need. His whole calendar filled up in an instant, and he was so busy he forgot to sing. He forgot about being happy.

Watching from his window, the rich man waited to hear the poor man's usual joyful singing. He heard nothing, but only saw the poor man calculating. When he saw what the gold did to the other man's joy, it occurred to the rich man that all his own efforts to amass money in order to gain happiness actually defeated that purpose. He had set out hoping to find happiness, but in the process of pursuing it, happiness got lost along the way.

Our Relationship to Things

The priority we give to material goods in our life is up to each of us to determine. This is also part of deciding how we want to define ourselves. If we are looking to our jobs and to material things to tell us how we are, what we are worth, and where we fit in the world, this is a sign that we have become profoundly confused about the order of things. It shows we have missed the point about how we human beings stand in relation to the material world.

Recently in Tibet, it became a popular fashion trend to wear tiger and leopard skins. Some rich people started the fashion, and then it became a matter of competing to keep up with them. People began outdoing each other in draping themselves with these expensive furs. In earlier times, it had been forbidden for common people to wear the skins of such animals, so it seems that people who wanted to damage Tibetan culture were encouraging Tibetans to wear such furs as a sign of defiance against the old Tibetan ways. His Holiness the Dalai Lama appealed to Tibetans not to wear these furs, saying it was a non-Tibetan, nonvirtuous practice.

We might see a similar kind of crowd mentality on a smaller scale, even within a single family. In a household where everyone eats meat, one vegetarian will often succumb to eating meat. Everyone has the right to their own way of thinking and to uniquely be who they are. Yet we often think it is sufficient to imitate others, and so for superficial reasons we end up surrendering our right to make our own decisions. It is worth observing our own consumer behavior to see if we ourselves have fallen into this kind of mindless conformism.

Time to Be Happy

I grew up in a very remote part of Tibet, far from the developed world. There were virtually no consumer goods in the entire area. Many people think of such remote places as backward. Where I lived, people only worked a few hours a day. When there was work that needed to be done, they worked. When there was no work to be done, they relaxed. Most people might see us as lazy, but we were generally quite happy. Family members had time to enjoy each other's company. People spent time in the day sitting together to eat, and in the evenings we gathered by the fire to tell stories.

Life in the city is different. People do not look at what work needs to be done; they look at the clock to tell them what to do. We let the clock run our life. Even if it is not the time for work, we carry with us the feeling that there must be some work we should be doing, and so we look for something to keep ourselves busy. This is a sign that we are no longer thinking for ourselves about what we actually need to be doing in order to be happy. It is a sign that we need to look away from the clock and look within.

We human beings are the ones who have engineered the goods and placed the labels on everything in the world. This should mean that we are in charge. But instead, somehow we feel that as long as the machines are running, we have to run along beside them. It seems to me that we have actually made ourselves slaves to what we ourselves created. This misuse of our own intelligence is harming us deeply. We have to regain our perspective and our balance. We need to recognize where these fabricated goods and fabricated identities come from.

In the end, it is up to each of us to determine what money and the things that money buys are really worth to us. It is up to us to decide how much energy to devote to the pursuit of money and possessions, as opposed to the pursuit of real happiness.

Do you want to let yourself be defined by your possessions or by your job? I mean this as a serious question, because you could identify yourself with your job or your money or your possessions. Or you could identify yourself with your inner qualities and with happiness. It really is up to you.

The Greatest Wealth: Contentment

As I have mentioned, there are healthy and unhealthy ways to relate to our possessions. I truly feel that contentment is the greatest wealth. Anyone can claim it for themselves. Anyone can own it. Contentment is an incredible wealth that we don't have to pay for, or seek anywhere outside ourselves. The natural resources to create this wealth are the inner riches of our own mind. Contentment is a wealth that gives the highest satisfaction, and we can gain it simply by mining our own mental resources, and knowing our own mind. We can cultivate the perspective that what we have is enough. We can see that we do not actually need more than we already have, and can be completely satisfied with that.

Normally we believe that we need so many conditions and so many things in order to be happy. But maybe it is actually very simple. This suddenly dawned on me one day as I was going for a walk around the monastery. It was a pleasant day, and there was a gentle breeze. This triggered in my mind the awareness of my breath. I became aware of these simple facts: I was breathing, and this was not something that depended on me alone. It depended on the presence of oxygen in the air—and a thousand prior steps had to take place in order for the oxygen to be there for me when I needed to take a single breath.

I was struck with a complete sense of wonder at this thought. I knew I could not make oxygen on my own. Yet my very survival depended on it being available to me for each breath. I have breathed a countless number of times, and if at any one time the oxygen had been missing, my life could have ended. Yet here it was, and always has been. This filled me with a complete and total sense of well-being.

The most ordinary things can be so amazing. We almost never turn our awareness to the basic conditions for our own existence, yet they are constantly present and freely available. Just recalling this at any moment can bring back the sense of joy I felt then.

We do not need to buy or own anything in order to be happy. At any moment, we can access this sense of joy. The same interdependence that makes our consumerism so devastating for the environment can also make the natural environment a source of endless joy and wonder to us, without taking away anything more than a lungful of air. It just depends on how we choose to live our connectedness.

I guess in the end it comes down to our attitude. The moment we stop letting greed make us chase after what we do not have and take for granted all that we do have, we can feel a deep and joyful sense of appreciation. We truly have everything we need already. The inexhaustible wealth of contentment is there waiting. We can find boundless happiness in simply breathing.

6 ◆ Social Action
Caring for All

LOOKING AT CONSUMER CULTURE and the greed that drives it, we may find a great deal in our societies that we would like to change. It is important not only to identify what we dislike and want to leave behind, but also to have a positive vision of what we would like to see in its place. Once we have such a vision, it is up to each of us to find the specific area where we can make our own contributions to making this vision a reality. What I would like to offer here is a way to orient ourselves toward creating a better world, no matter what sort of social action we engage in.

Social action is a particular way of caring for others. The fact that human beings live together in societies is proof that we need one another's care. Our dependence on one another has practical as well as ethical implications for the social institutions we build. Because we are all profoundly interconnected, one person's well-being is intimately connected to the well-being of the rest of their community. If we create social systems that honor our basic interconnectedness, our society will be aligned with the reality of our existence. This will give us the basis for a society that is stable, and also supportive of human happiness.

To get a clearer vision of the society we wish to create, I suggest that we think in terms of placing happiness at the center. We could begin to conceive of lasting happiness as the most important product our country or society can produce. This might lead us to consider certain questions, such as: What sort of personal qualities do we want to see our society encouraging in its members? What sort of relationships should our society foster between people in order to create more happiness?

We have seen that competition and greed bring neither happiness nor meaning in life. We can imagine what our society would look like instead if it drew primarily on the human qualities of compassion and love rather than on our potential for greed. We can envision a society designed to connect us as friends and close communities, rather than pit us against each other as competitors. Then we can ask what action is needed in order to move our society in that direction.

Once you have a clear vision of the values you wish to support and the change you wish to see, you will find many social issues to work on. You can choose to act in whatever area your talents and interests take you, with the confidence that all social issues are ultimately interconnected. Any positive impact you make on one issue will have far-reaching consequences, because all aspects of life are interconnected.

Affection Is Not Optional

Living in a society should be our daily reminder of how much we receive from and owe to one another. A clear awareness of this debt for the kindness we receive from others can provide a stable foundation for engagement in social service or activism. Our actions can be grounded in the simple wish to care for others as we ourselves have been cared for by the world.

You may feel that you do not owe anything to anyone because you paid for what you use. But everything you have still comes to you through the efforts of others; you just might need to make an effort to recognize this. You did not chop trees to make the paper this book is printed on, or create the network that delivered it to you. But you are now enjoying the fruits of the labor of those who did so. In my own case, I receive a great deal from others all the time. Because I am a Buddhist monk, my vows require that literally everything I have is offered to me as a donation by others—my food, my clothes, the books in my library, everything.

In my present situation, I have nothing tangible to give back to anyone. People often come to see me with high hopes for what I can do for them. Mostly I have one simple thing to give: from my heart I offer them my love and my hopes for their happiness. Even when there is little else I can offer, I truly wish to know the answer when I ask, "How are you? How do you feel? How is your mind? Are you well these days?"

In earlier times, there seemed to be a genuine concern when asking, "How are you?" Now, this often seems like a mere formality. People might not have any real interest in hearing the answer to that question. Instead, what they really want to know is: "How is your business going? How much are you worth? What can you do for me?" Though there may be nothing tangible I can do for the people I meet, I can concern myself with their well-being. In a world where so little importance is placed on genuinely caring for others, and where true love and compassion seem to be rare, maybe this can have some value. The fact that there is one person in the world who cares and feels love for them does seem to touch people deeply. In a world of too little love, I can see that even just that simple expression of love makes a deep impression on people. It brings some real happiness.

Just asking and earnestly waiting to hear how people feel entails a very small shift in behavior. But it could help us cultivate a habit of connecting heart to heart, and of sincerely caring for others. I think that on a larger scale, too, the attitude of inquiring and listening attentively to what others feel and need forms a sound basis for any social action. It is a way to ensure that love infuses all that we do to benefit others.

I mentioned earlier in chapter 4, "Gender Identities," that I feel the world needs to make a global shift in its values, to favor the ability to listen rather than the ability to make assertions. We can contribute to this shift as social activists by listening carefully before developing any plan to act. This helps ensure that our activism is truly attentive to others' well-being and experience of happiness, and not simply an imposition of our views. We can begin to train ourselves in a small way, by just waiting to truly hear the answer whenever we ask: How are you?

It is important to recognize that love, concern, and affection are not optional. We do not need any reason to offer love and affection. It is possible to have love without prices and without conditions. We do not need any further compensation beyond just giving our love. And love is an infinitely renewable resource. For the well-being of society and for our own personal growth as well, it is crucial that we learn to love without needing a reason or reward.

When you feel authentic love toward others, you will be deeply moved to act. You will not rest until you have found ways to secure the happiness of all those you are able to include in your feelings of love. As you learn to love more and more widely, your love will motivate you to act to benefit not just the few people in your inner circle, but your whole society, and eventually, the whole world. This makes love an immensely powerful basis for social action of any sort. As I will discuss in chapter 11, "Sustainable Compassion," basing our social action in compassion and love will make it sustainable over the long run as well.

Backward or Forward?

In order to define the direction in which we want to see our society shift, we need to be willing to challenge the prevailing ideas of what constitutes social progress. I have some personal experience to share with you in this regard. From the perspective of the relatively developed Chinese to our east, people living in the remote part of Tibet where I was born were commonly described as "backward." We were held to be failures. It is true that we had no grocery stores and no factories. But now that I have been exposed to the "developed world," when I look back on that way of life, I wonder if we were so backward. We worked enough to have food and clothes and to meet our other basic requirements, and we did not worry about what else we did not have. From what I observed, people in my isolated part of Tibet had what they needed, and they were happy.

This makes me wonder: In terms of satisfaction in life, might it be the developed world that is lagging behind traditional societies like the nomadic community I was born in? When people first left Tibet as refugees and encountered the modernized world, they were relatively simple, straightforward, and good-hearted, but were looked down upon as people who didn't fit in. It seems that in "advanced" societies, the less straightforward you are—the more clever and manipulative—the more you fit in and even rise to the top. We have to question the sanity of this sort of system. If gaining access to more material resources in such a way is considered to be progress, things seem completely upside down to me.

Are we willing to accept that having more wealth—no matter how someone acquires it—is a sign of being more advanced? Surely there are other measures we could use to determine whether we have enough, besides comparing ourselves with those who happen to have amassed more money and things than we have. If the measure of success is having more than the other people around us, this is a recipe for failure. Competing with others simply cannot bring real happiness. Even if happiness did come from being the best and having the most, ultimately only one person in the world—the one with the most—could ever be truly happy or "successful." Everyone else would be condemned to failure.

I think we have to be very careful not to confuse economic success with personal happiness. Just because we have a market economy does not mean we need to have a market society. We can find ways to relate to each other on different principles than business ones. We could define development in terms of how much we are able to increase bonds of friendship and closeness, and by how central we make community and mutual affection. When I think of a society that creates happiness, I think of a society where compassion and love replace competition and greed as the emotional forces that bind us together.

Once we have redefined for ourselves the values we wish to place at the heart of society, we can look at particular social institutions and issues, and ask what needs to be changed. We will have the orientation we need to enact our aspirations in whatever area of social action we choose.

Caring for All

It often seems to me that all over the globe, our priorities have become very confused. The most important things that we need in order to support life have been turned into commodities. Basic needs like health care, nutritional food, and shelter are seen as optional luxuries for people who can afford them. Other people's welfare seems completely dispensable. These distorted principles are at work in many of the social systems we have created. This is rooted in profound ignorance. It arises from a failure to truly see that everyone is exactly equal in wanting to be happy and to be free of suffering. Happiness is a fundamental right of any human being.

Equality and interdependence are both basic principles underlying our existence as human beings. When we fail to recognize this, we end up subjecting our relations with our fellow human beings to business principles: If you give me something, I'll care for you. If I get nothing from you, I won't care. I am not describing something that could happen to human society. I am describing what *is* happening in many social institutions. What should be basic rights are treated as marketable items, and therefore enter into the back-and-forth of commercial exchange. We seem to have lost the sense that we can freely and happily extend ourselves for others. In modeling our social institutions on business principles, we have become very disconnected from our own noble heart.

For example, from what I have heard, it seems that many health-care systems around the world are run on business models. I am told that in America, when people arrive in the emergency room, even if they are in terrible pain, the first question they are asked is not about their injury or medical condition. It is about their insurance. If you have insurance, they will ease your pain and care for you. If not, you either prove that you have money to pay, or go somewhere else. While I do not pretend to have solutions to all the complex political and economic issues at work in the health-care industry, still it is very difficult to fathom how we reached the point where this seems an acceptable way of treating our fellow human beings.

Health care may be complicated in America, but health-care systems are malfunctioning all around the world. Europe, Africa, Asia, and Australia all have their own problems. Here in India, some of the better hospitals require a cash deposit before they will give you a bed. Recently, a woman here died in childbirth just outside the doors of a hospital that had denied her entry because she had no money.

Reliable health care is often not just expensive—it can be simply unavailable. In many parts of the world, cars are easier to attain than health care. Everything is done to bring down the price of cars and gasoline, so that as many people as possible can afford to buy and maintain a car. If you need gas, there are gas stations right beside the road everywhere you go. If you have a flat tire, there are places every few blocks where you can get it fixed. But when you have a health emergency and need to get to a hospital, though it would be easy to find a car, get it washed, pump its tires, and refill its gas tank, it can be very difficult to find a good hospital to drive to. Even once you reach the hospital, getting the care you need for your body is much harder than getting service for your car. I would hope that physical health is more important than cars, but it doesn't seem so, judging from the way society has prioritized caring for cars rather than people's health.

The example of health-care systems is a powerful indication that business concerns top the list of priorities in most societies. Freedom is way down on the list. Real happiness may not even be on the list! When we cease to value happiness, we are living in a society that is denying the worth of human life, because human beings have the potential to experience real, lasting happiness. Society should do all it can to enable us to live up to that potential, by offering real conditions for happiness. Love and compassion are conducive to human happiness; competition and greed are not. I believe that a society that does not support the conditions of real happiness is failing to respect the value of human life.

Imagining instead a society that values human life and its potential for happiness, we can ask ourselves: What kind of health-care systems would we create if we retained an awareness of the pain and suffering of the people seeking care? This awareness would not be hard to create. All human beings are alike in their experience of the feelings of pain and pleasure. Our capacity to experience joy as well as sorrow, pleasure as well as pain, and our ever-present longing to be free of suffering—these are common to us all. This means we each have a solid basis for empathizing with everyone else.

Although we do not directly perceive other people's feelings of physical pain, based on our own body we can easily get a clear sense of what others are feeling. We can bridge the physical gap between self and other with a simple act of imagination. When we develop the habit of imagining ourselves in another person's place, we will easily recognize our equality. We will find it unacceptable to let others suffer, because we recognize that we share with them the same capacity for suffering.

The potential for happiness is something all human beings also share. Our fundamental equality means that no one has a greater or lesser claim than anyone else to be happy and free of pain. This awareness of equality should be a guiding principle in building a compassionate society.

Difference without Division

At the same time, recognizing our human equality should not prevent us from acknowledging our social and cultural differences. Just because we are equal does not mean we have to be identical. Nor do our cultural differences undermine our equal rights to happiness, nor our rights to equal access to basic services such as health care and education, which are a necessity for all human beings alike. Social systems need to take both our equality and our differences into account.

Diversity within a society does not have to be problematic; it can be a source of richness and enjoyment. We can recognize and enjoy differences, but we must be careful not to exaggerate their importance or solidify our differences. When we do, we easily lose sight of our shared humanity, and divide ourselves up into categories of us and them, higher and lower, better and worse.

In the Tibetan community in exile, these patterns are widespread. Among Tibetans in India, we see major differences in the viewpoint and behavior of newcomers versus those of oldtimers—that is, between Tibetans who have recently arrived in India, and those who came to India fifty years ago or were born outside Tibet. Among Tibetans from Tibet in particular, there are those who cling to regional identities based on which of the three Tibetan provinces they came from. There is no problem with coming from different places. The problem arises when we stick a label on people based on place, and treat that label as if it were part of them.

For example, when we Tibetans hear that a person comes from the province of Amdo in Tibet, if we ourselves are not from Amdo, then we feel that this person is not part of our group. This is how a difference is made into a means of separation. But this is unnecessary. When we hear that someone is from a different place than we are, that could be a reason for us to draw them closer and to take greater interest in them. Perhaps people from Amdo have been exposed to things we have not experienced. They might have some new perspectives to share. Knowing them could enrich our view of the world, and even our understanding of life.

However, this enrichment will not happen if we believe we already know what people from Amdo are like. We hear that someone is from such and such a place, and we stick to our own small set of associations. This becomes a label that we believe represents the essential aspects of the group, without knowing much about its individual members as human beings at all. Once this happens, we are closed to learning anything new from them or even about them. We make them something separate from us, and so it can even become difficult to connect with them, since we have already shut them off in a box.

The example of Muslims might be more familiar. When we think of Muslims, one thing immediately comes to many people's minds: terrorism. We don't think about the great cultures of Islam. There is no thought of the great art, architecture, literature, or philosophies—just terrorism. We take isolated bits of information, and apply them generally to everyone in that group. The information we think of as most important is seldom really the most important. That information may not be accurate at all, and even when it is, it never reflects the whole picture. Nor will it apply to everyone in the group.

We should immediately distrust statements like, "Such and such group of people are all terribly backward," or they are "all" thieves, or "all" anything. No group of human beings is ever homogenous. Even a single individual is internally diverse, full of varying thoughts and emotions at different moments. Reflecting on this, we can make a conscious decision to cultivate greater wisdom in our understanding of other individuals and communities. We can start by questioning how complete or relevant our ideas about others are. We can also decide that we will seek out what is positive in our differences. We can do this by simply focusing on what is good in the other group. We can value how we might be enriched, and what we might learn if we look at life from their perspectives. If nothing else, we can simply ask them what special food dishes they have, or what the beautiful places in their region are like. Learning to appreciate differences can start with something as simple as that.

Valuing Diversity

My personal view is that human diversity is very much to be welcomed. If we take our body as an analogy, our eyes are obviously different from our nose and limbs and mouth. They look different, and their functions are different. But they are all parts of the same body. Each has an important role to play, and they are all mutually supporting. Even if we do not immediately see their connections, it is clear that the parts do all function together, with each making a distinct contribution to the whole.

I have a story about this; I hope you do not find it too earthy. As this story goes, there was a meeting of all the important parts of the body. The purpose of the meeting was to determine which part was the most important. All the body's bigwigs were invited: the lungs, liver, kidneys, heart, intestines, the bones—basically, everybody who was anybody. But they didn't invite the anus to their meeting. When he realized that he had been left out of this council of all the body parts, he took it very personally. How could they deny he was part of their team? Deeply offended, he decided to go on strike.

Oh, how the rest of the parts suffered when all the traffic got blocked! They no longer felt so high and mighty. The other parts of the body all had to come begging the anus's forgiveness, asking him to join the meeting and resume his very important activities. When the meeting resumed, lo and behold, they voted unanimously in favor of the anus as the most important. So, no matter what people think: no one is insignificant.

There is no hierarchy in a body. All the parts are mutually dependent and mutually supportive. Likewise, we human beings are all parts of the same body. Just because we do not wish to acknowledge another person's importance does not mean that this person is unimportant to our well-being. Just because we do not wish to acknowledge what we share with others does not mean that we can separate ourselves from them. Interdependence is an inescapable truth of our existence.

Of course, we are not all identical. Because certain differences do exist between us, we all have something to offer each other. We can work together making our diverse and complementary contributions. Because we are all part of the same social body, it is in our own best interest to assure that we can all function well together.

A Global Society

The society we live in today is global. People leave their homes and seek opportunities in distant countries, and as a result, we are likely to be sharing our community with people of different cultures and nationalities. Immigration is another indication of the global dimension of our interdependence.

The presence of immigrants can be a test case for compassion in many societies. We can see this at work in the United States, and in other wealthy nations in the Persian Gulf states and within Western Europe as well. Immigration is a test of a society's commitment to real human equality in the face of apparent human differences. It brings home—very literally—the ethical implications of interdependence and equality. What will you do when people leave their own homes because they were suffering there, and move right into your neighborhood in search of happiness? When such people depend on you for kindness and compassion, do you allow their ethnicity or citizenship to become a pretext for creating boundaries between them and yourself?

We could look at the case of immigrants to see how we should apply the basic values our society upholds. If we do, I think we will recognize that no matter where immigrants come from, they all yearn to be happy just as we do. They have the same basic human right to happiness. We may not be able to understand all of the complex social issues that underlie people's decision to leave their homes behind. Yet we can say with certainty that most people who immigrate to more prosperous nations do so in pursuit of better conditions for happiness.

I know that many Tibetan refugees try to immigrate to the United States in hopes of better opportunities. Many lack the benefits of education, special professional skills, or wealth. There is no guarantee they will find a better life when they arrive, but they place all their highest hopes on America. Whole families pool their resources to help one member reach their goal. Years are spent considering and planning this major move. After deciding to leave everything that is familiar to them, many immigrants risk everything they have, and undergo terrible hardship to get to the place of their hopes. I think before anyone takes such a step, they must truly have exhausted all other options in their home country.

In some cases, if illegal immigrants are sent back to their home countries, their life is finished. Perhaps the tightest border in the world today is the one between North Korea and South Korea. Many North Koreans who want to leave their country manage to cross the border into China. When China sends them back, it is sending them back to certain suffering. Escaping from Tibet also involves serious risks. When I fled Tibet, I was aware that if I was caught I would face certain imprisonment, or worse. This was a terrifying experience, and it is shared by countless other immigrants.

Of course, for any country, it is difficult to just welcome in all those who want to enter. For one, resources are limited. National security is another issue. Yet immigration is also, and perhaps primarily, a human issue. Immigration laws may be cut-and-dried, but people's lives are not cut-and-dried. There is no easy answer about open or closed borders. But either way, there remains the challenge of finding help for desperate people.

Who will lead if not America? The people who run the government must recall that, originally, all Americans were immigrants. Their ancestors first arrived in the United States because of a lack of opportunity and freedom in their original homes. These are the ideals symbolized by America's Statue of Liberty. Doesn't it say, "Give me your tired, your poor, your huddled masses yearning to breathe free"? This is a truly noble ideal that Americans could pay tribute to today by helping others find hope. These are ideals that the rest of the world should embrace as well.

Many of the most vulnerable people who move into new countries end up performing functions that those there before them do not want to do for themselves. Even if immigrants seem to occupy the bottom rungs of society, this only shows that they form part of the foundation supporting the rest of society. They perform services that citizens use and need. In fact, their labor keeps the prices of many goods and services affordable, and helps keep the national economy competitive with other nations. Whether legal or illegal, there is no denying that immigrants form an integral part of the entire social organism, and contribute a great deal to it. Yet the people who immigrate are entirely at the mercy of others. Whether or not we have a legal obligation, we have a clear and unequivocal human obligation to care for them.

I think the issues involved in immigration apply well beyond the discussions of how to treat a country's immigrants. They raise broader questions: How do we acknowledge our equality with those who serve us? How do we respond to those whose misfortune makes them willing to work for wages we would never deign to accept? How can we even begin to repay this debt that we owe to those whose suffering makes our own lifestyle affordable and easy?

In fact, whether or not they have a large immigrant population, many societies in the world today are dependent on the cheap labor of citizens of other countries. Those workers might live in our country, or they may be working in other countries. In either case, the fact remains that we are benefiting from their labor and the suffering that it involves, however near or far they may be. We are all participating in a global society and a global economy. This should remind us that our responsibility to care for others is itself global. Our responsibility is universal.

Open Field for Action

If we take a clear sense of our values with us wherever we go, we will find a vast scope for enacting our vision of a better society. In the next two chapters, I will focus on two other areas that offer many opportunities for us to engage in social action—environmental protection and food justice. Yet in whatever area we choose to act, once we have an idea of what we would like our society to become, we can aspire and act to make that vision a reality. We can take our own best aspirations, and engage in social action based on them. We do not need to go out and find new aspirations. We can keep all our aspirations, and just apply them as we work for the benefit of all.

If you act on that basis, then what you do is full of meaning, regardless of how many outer results you show. The fact that you have the intention to work for others is important. Act on your wholesome intentions and altruistic impulses. If you have the thought of benefiting society, that is significant. Nurture and treasure that thought, and act on it as best you can. Doing so will certainly change you, and that in itself can be the start of the change you want to see in your world.

7 • Environmental Protection

*Cultivating New Feelings for
the Earth*

AS WE LOOK FOR WAYS to enact our vision of a more compassionate society, one area crying out for attention is our treatment of our natural environment. Protecting the environment that we all rely on for our survival is an immediate way to care for all beings.

We have seen that the global culture of consumerism that has been so devastating for our planet stems from an emotional force that creeps into human hearts—the force of greed. In that and other ways, human attitudes and feelings are causing large-scale destruction of our physical environment. Therefore our efforts to protect the environment are best effected by making changes to our attitudes and feelings.

In recent years, we have gained a great deal of information about the impact of our actions on the environment. We human beings have tremendous intelligence, but it is clear that there remains a big gap between the brain and the heart. We seem to find it easy to process new information and generate new ideas, yet much harder to produce new feelings. Although we readily recognize the import of a situation conceptually, somehow this understanding often fails to move our heart. Our intellectual intelligence doesn't transfer into intelligent emotions, and our heart and brain seem to remain a world apart. What we now need to go along with all our powerful new ideas about the environment are powerful new feelings.

There are ways of thinking about the earth that go beyond just acquiring knowledge, and actually lead us to feel deeply for our physical environment. A sense of wonder and appreciation of the earth's beauty is a helpful place to start in developing strong feelings for the environment. When we talk about the environment, in broadest terms we are talking about the whole universe. Studying astronomy can reveal just how magnificent the universe is, and studying earth sciences reveals the magnificence of our particular home in this vast universe. In my own case, I found great affinities between the study of the environment and Buddhism. Each helped deepen my understanding of the other; each enlivened my feeling for the other.

I have noticed that sometimes people speak of our planet as a thing. This attitude will not lead to the feelings of closeness and affection that would move us to take care of the earth. As we know, the earth is not a dead rock floating in space. It is a living system, in itself as a whole and in each and every part. I do not see the earth as an inanimate object—a lump of stone. I think of it as being alive. Sitting on the earth, I feel that I am resting on a mother's lap. It is thanks to her that everything exists. In this way, we could easily think of the earth as a goddess—a living, breathing, and constantly giving goddess.

The Stage That Sustains All

I do not believe we can ever possibly be too grateful to the earth. It is the universal home where we have experienced every phase of all our lives, in the past, now, and in the future. In this way, the earth offers herself equally to us all, as the stage on which to act out our happiness and our sorrows—our most joyful comedies and our most heart-wrenching tragedies, and everything in between. Yet the reality is that we are rapidly destroying her. If the only platform we have collapses, all the present and future acts of our lives will be over, forever.

I think the earth can be a teacher to us, offering a model of how to care for and treat others. She especially shows us how to see everyone as completely equal. In conventional terms, we speak of good people and bad people. Our society praises those considered "good," and shuns or even banishes those considered "bad." The earth never does this, ever. To her, we are all the same. She does not make a distinction, but instead grants us all alike the conditions we need to survive and live out our lives.

Even if people whom society condemns as "bad guys" were exiled, they could not live on the moon, could they? The most hardened criminals can count on the same support and acceptance that our mother, the earth, offers the holiest of saints. She offers the same air to all beings alike, unconditionally. She shows us what it means to be enduring, accommodating, and providing. She never gives up on us.

We have a Buddhist prayer in which we ourselves aspire to become like her. We say:

> May I be like the earth,
> providing the air, the ground, water,
> and everything she provides
> that is our sacred source of life.

Inspired by the example of the earth, this prayer encourages us to aspire to be an unconditional source of all well-being and life for others. This is a supreme aspiration. We do not just have a great deal to learn about the environment—we also have a lot to learn from it.

Deep Ecology, Deep Respect

In traditional Tibetan culture, religion, and philosophy, there is a deeply rooted respect for nature. Nature is sacred. Our relationship to nature is similar to what is found in Native American cultures. Traditional Tibetans believe the mountains and streams are inhabited by divine beings. When they see an impressive tree or rock, they feel it is bound to be the abode of a sacred spirit.

In traditional Tibet, we would not even dream of polluting a water source that was used by other people or animals. We believed we would incur the wrath of the sacred spirits dwelling in that river or mountain. The fireplace was also held to be sacred. Nothing could be burned in it other than clean fuel, not even wool. The smoke of burning wool may not be toxic, but it was said that its smoke would disturb some spirit beings. For that reason, we would never burn wool, so you can obviously forget about burning plastic!

Where I grew up, we were completely isolated from modern "conveniences"—no electricity, no cars, not even bicycles. This was the sort of place where a few pieces of candy caused tremendous excitement. If as a child you managed to get three pieces of candy in a year, you were having a very good year. Apart from those three candy wrappers, we did not even see plastic from one year to the next. We did not particularly have to worry about what to do with our waste, because there was virtually nothing that was not biodegradable.

I guess the nomadic area where I grew up was one of the very last places where our ancient Tibetan culture was still alive. Everything has changed now. In the years since I left there, the Chinese authorities strongly urged people to settle in houses, buy motorcycles, and participate in the larger cash economy. The way of life I knew then has all but disappeared. But I am truly very happy to have been able to experience it directly for myself. I am deeply grateful for that.

The sense of nature as sacred has supported the feelings of caring and closeness to the environment that have been with me my whole life. When I was four or five years old, a source of water in our valley began to dry up. For nomads in an arid zone with large flocks to care for, this was a very serious matter. The loss of a water source would have a huge impact on our lives. It was a common belief in our area that planting trees helped protect water sources. What we learn now in science class about watersheds was simply handed down then as part of our ancestral wisdom. I planted a tree near that dwindling spring, with my father. Actually, he did most of the work, small as I was, but I remember saying prayers at that time for all living beings in the area to have water. In that high altitude and harsh climate, it is hard for trees to survive, but this one did, and so did our spring. I think my heartfelt wish to care for the environment began from that time.

Awakening the Feeling in Others

When I left Tibet, I carried with me those feelings toward the natural environment. Later, as an adult, I decided to organize a conference in the city of Varanasi, India, in order to educate Buddhist monks and nuns on environmental issues. For most of them, this was their first exposure to the topic, and I saw that the monks and nuns attending that conference were deeply affected—not just intellectually stimulated, but emotionally moved. Seeing that people could become inspired to act to protect the environment encouraged me to do more in the area of environmental activism. Not everyone has grown up in a situation where respect for the sanctity of nature is nurtured from childhood, but I saw that it is possible to instill this feeling of respect and awe for the environment later in life, too. That gave me the courage to try to do more.

Unlike the Tibetan monastics in Himalayan monasteries and nunneries, most people in the West receive extensive education in environmental awareness as a matter of course. You have already been exposed to a great deal of information about the effects of pollution, global warming, and the overall effects of our long-term abuse of our planet. I do not think I need to tell you how urgently we need to take steps to protect our home.

Maybe the better place to start is by discussing how. The single most important factor that will move us to act to protect the world is compassion. Our compassion must encompass all that is inanimate as well as animate. In fact, it may at times be difficult to distinguish between what is animate and inanimate, but our compassion should extend to both the physical environment and the beings that inhabit it.

True Fearlessness

Compassion is central to environmental protection because it moves us to act to cherish and take care of others. Caring for the environment is an important way to care for all the beings that depend on it for their existence. Compassion involves more than simply knowing about a difficult situation.

Even witnessing pain directly does not necessarily prompt a reaction of compassion. I observed this for myself once while watching a documentary in which animals were being hung upside down to be slaughtered. As their throats were cut, blood spurted out and their legs jerked in terror and pain. It was extremely hard to watch—unbearable, really. But as the butchers sawed through the animals' necks to deprive them of life, the men were laughing and joking. They could obviously see the animals' painful movements and hear their cries—the suffering was visible and audible—but they did not seem to recognize that these were signs of terrible pain. And even if the butchers did see that they were inflicting pain, the animals' suffering didn't amount to anything for them. They treated it as if they were watching a show.

In fact, some people even kill animals as a form of recreation. Hunting is considered a sport in some cultures, isn't it? Some people seem to believe it is courageous to kill animals. Unfortunately, nowadays we have developed the wrong kind of fearlessness—fearlessness in harming others. At some point, this "courage" in harming others is bound to turn on us. As people become habituated to taking the life of animals with no thought for the pain they are causing, in the end it becomes easy to harm and kill humans. Even the pain of our fellow human beings can cease to catch our attention.

The real courage that comes from compassion is very far from this. When compassion is present, we do not overlook others' pain. Rather, there is a sense of urgency to end that pain, as if a fire has just been lit underneath you. When you have such compassion, as soon as you see suffering, you wish to jump up and act to end it at once. You have no fear and no hesitation in taking on the suffering of other people, animals, and even the planet itself. This is what I would call the right kind of fearlessness. This is the fearlessness of true heroes.

I think what is missing in those who see others' pain but feel nothing is a sense of closeness, and a recognition of just how similar we and other living beings really are. When these qualities are lacking, even actions to benefit others might not actually be rooted in compassion. Compassionate action does not imply looking down on some poor, pitiful animal or person, and showering our charity on them from a lofty position above. That kind of charitable action can end up just feeding our ego, and can be more like a savior complex or pride than actual compassion. With that kind of pitying attitude, we are actually holding ourselves apart from other beings. We are denying our profound similarity to them.

Real compassion is wholly unlike this. With compassion, we come closer to other living beings as we recognize that they are vulnerable to suffering, just as we are. By applying our own experiences of suffering to what we see in others, we feel something akin to what they are feeling. This pierces our heart and becomes unbearable, and generates an intense resolve to do something right away to protect them. True compassion translates directly into action.

Misunderstandings about Compassion

Compassion is a powerful tool in our work to protect the environment. We need compassion because it connects us personally to the issue, and sustains us over the long haul. Some people misunderstand this point, and say they don't want to feel compassion. They assume compassion will add to their own suffering, because they think it involves personally feeling the pain they see around them. This may happen especially when people contemplate the widespread destruction of our wildlife and the environment as a whole. "This is too much," they may say. "I have enough problems of my own. I can't take on any more."

This reflects a misunderstanding of the nature of compassion. Compassion is what we feel when we focus on the person or animal who is suffering, not what we feel when we focus only on the suffering. What is the object of your compassion? It is the being who is suffering. If you take an animal or person as the object of your compassion, you will not be overwhelmed by their suffering. If your attention is not directed primarily at the suffering, you can focus on them, and on what you can do for them.

Imagine if something you value and treasure were to fall into a fire. You would not focus on the heat and the flames that were consuming it. Keenly feeling the object's value and wanting to protect it, you would focus on the object, and immediately use whatever you found at hand to try to save it from the fire. You would not agonize over how hot the fire was, or how sad the situation was, or sit there contemplating whether you really had the right tool. Nor would you focus on yourself. Your concern to safeguard the object would prevent you from indulging in any self-interested thoughts. You would just take in the information that you needed in order to resolve the situation, and act.

The point is to care so keenly for others that you give rise to courage and determination to relieve them of their suffering. That is compassion.

Another misunderstanding is that compassion is something you now lack, so you need to go out and get it from somewhere. When we are talking about compassion, we are not talking about something that is foreign to us, needing to be imported. Rather, compassion is inherent in every person, as an integral part of us throughout the day, every day.

The fact that you have affection for your family members or pets is due to the compassion and love that already lie within you. Even your wish to tend the garden outside your window is an expression of love and caring. Compassion is not something new that you need to acquire and plant. It is a question only of nurturing the seeds you already have.

Transferring Care to Others

Confusion can arise due to certain similarities between compassion and attachment. Both involve a kind of caring, although in other ways they are radically different. Attachment is aimed at our own interests, and involves caring about ourselves. Compassion is aimed at others' interests, and has to do with caring for others.

This similarity is something we can make use of in our spiritual lives. Here is a simple example: Let's say you have three pieces of fruit. If you eat them all yourself and do not share any with others, that is attachment or desire. It involves caring only for oneself. However, if you eat one and give the remaining two to others to enjoy, it can become compassion. Attachment or desire will have been transformed into caring for others. In this way, compassion is a sort of transfer of yourself to others.

It is true that we all have a certain measure of desire, or attachment, but we also have the ability to transform this into compassion. However, as an extreme form of attachment, the greed we were discussing earlier poses a serious obstacle to our cultivation of compassion. I hope it is clear by now how important it is for us to break the spell of greed that we have fallen under—and guard against its recurrence once the spell is broken.

To that end, we can actively heighten our awareness of our fundamental dependence on others and on the environment. As we recognize more and more clearly how deeply interdependent we all are on one another, our sense of closeness to others and to the earth can likewise deepen. A profound awareness of interdependence weakens our sense of separation and difference, and can ultimately eliminate it. This provides a powerful support for our efforts to transform attachment's caring about self into compassion's caring for the world.

Letting the Heart Lead

We began this discussion of the environment by noting that although we have many sound new ideas about the environment, they are often not accompanied by sound new emotions. Without developing healthy emotions, we will not have all of the resources we need in order to heal our planet. As a healthy emotion that we all can feel, compassion is one such resource.

I also pointed to the need to bring about a closer and healthier relationship between our intelligence and our emotions. We are often confused about which of the two we should prioritize. Sometimes it seems we value the intellect, but do not value emotions. In Buddhism, we speak of wisdom and compassion as necessarily paired. The healthy relationship between them is for compassion to be like a king, with wisdom or intelligence serving as its minister. The king commands, and the minister has to come up with a way to execute those commands. Similarly, our compassion should set the course of our actions, while our wisdom serves to determine how best to plot that course forward. In our case, too often the opposite is true. Intelligence is deployed indiscriminately, running all over the place, while compassion drags along far behind.

This is backward. We need to let the heart lead. Compassion is indispensable; it is the single most important factor we need if we are going to have any real success in protecting the environment, in creating a just society, or simply in living wholesome, happy lives.

Steps to Take

Once we are moved by a compassionate wish to care for the world—and have enough information about the state of the environment to see that change is needed—what is next? What can we actually do about it?

To avoid becoming overwhelmed by the enormity of the task at hand, it is important to keep in mind that society is nothing apart from its individual members. Our current environmental crisis was created by thousands of small acts, mostly done unthinkingly. It can also be undone by thousands of small acts—and if we engage in those acts consciously, problems can often be resolved more quickly than they were created.

I think it is important to identify clear steps that we can each take ourselves, here and now. Rethinking our personal consumption of meat is one way that we as individuals can have a direct impact. Vegetarianism involves many ethical issues, but it is also an issue of environmental protection. Our reliance on meat is a major cause of climate change, deforestation, and pollution. There is no shortage of facts to demonstrate this to us. Roughly 20 percent of the world's greenhouse gas emissions are caused by animals raised for human consumption. The methane gases emitted by livestock contribute more to climate change than does carbon dioxide. This tells us that if we human beings made a significant shift toward becoming vegetarian, by that shift alone we could dramatically reduce global warming.

As vegetarians, we would also make far more efficient use of what our planet offers us. Vast quantities of feed, water, land, fuel, and other resources are required to sustain livestock—far more than what is needed to produce a vegetarian diet. Studies indicate that the land needed to produce food for one meat-eater could support twenty vegetarians. This demonstrates how much smaller our ecological footprint could be just by giving up meat.

But we do not need scientists to demonstrate the pollution that is a direct by-product of the livestock industry. Just visiting a cattle or dairy farm—in fact, just driving past one and being hit by the smell—is enough to make viscerally clear what is being released into our environment. There is abundant information showing that our meat consumption is having an adverse effect on the environment.

The question is, what do we do about what these facts are telling us? Are we moved to take advantage of this huge opportunity we have to help slow climate change and reduce pollution by shifting away from meat?

There is also abundant information about the conditions under which animals raised for our food are living, how they are slaughtered, and what you are eating as a result of that. Even though we know there is intense suffering involved as well as devastating environmental consequences, many people still remain unswayed. Some people have taken note and responded accordingly, but most continue as before, as if nothing harmful were going on. Why?

Moving from Head to Heart

I want to share something personal with you. When I was young, I ate meat. In fact, I was notoriously fond of meat. (Luckily CNN wasn't there to cover it!) There were some local conditions that led to my meat eating. For one, I grew up in a remote place where people have to survive on what they have, and what we had was meat, butter, and Tibetan sweet cheese. These were the traditional foods, and there were few other foodstuffs available. Meat was simply what everyone ate, so based on those circumstances and through the sheer force of habit, we all ate meat.

Then I came to India. Six or seven years ago, I stopped eating meat. This happened after I watched a documentary about the meat industry. Seeing the images of animals being slaughtered made it simply unbearable for me to continue eating their flesh. Of course, I had contemplated becoming vegetarian before that, but it was only after seeing this documentary that I was moved to act.

This raises an important question: What does it take for our ideas to move our heart? In my case, the information was there, but it took quite a while until I actually felt that eating meat was impossible for me. What does it take to make that shift happen? How long must we wait until something we know is harmful becomes unbearable for us? Will we have to wait until the Pacific Ocean turns red with blood? Is this what it will take for the majority of people to wake up to what is going on? Even that might not have the necessary impact on our heart, because in fact, we already have plenty of compelling evidence to show us where our planet is headed.

Most people who would like to give up eating meat but have been unable to do so say the reason is because of the flavor and because of habit. Many people say they just like how meat tastes. What keeps them eating meat is craving the taste on their tongues. This is the power that emotions have in the face of our intellect. Because they are enslaved to their emotional craving for meat, many people do not want to give up meat even when they know that it is the right thing to do. Apart from that desire for the flavor, most people have no real reason to keep eating meat.

Now compare that reason to all the reasons why one should not eat meat—the ethical reasons, the health reasons, the spiritual reasons, and the many environmental reasons. These authentic reasons outweigh all others. It seems impossible that our small reasons for eating meat could survive in the face of the overwhelming abundance of reasons not to. Yet still we allow the tiny excuse of our taste buds to overshadow everything else. Even when we have a sound understanding of the relative merits of eating meat versus abstaining from it, even when we understand the impact of the livestock industry on the environment, we are not moved to follow the dictates of reason. It seems clear to me that we urgently need something that pierces our heart, and translates our ideas into feelings.

Building the Bridge

I had an experience that proved to me that it is possible to build the needed bridge between heart and mind. This took place in the winter of 2006 to 2007 in Bodh Gaya, India, the place where the Buddha was enlightened. Every year, three thousand to four thousand monks and nuns travel there from monasteries and nunneries across the Himalayas. Lay practitioners also come from all over the world, to pray together for world peace at our annual Kagyu Monlam gathering. During our last session, I decided to speak to all those gathered there about giving up meat.

I was not offering any new information on the matter. I had absolutely nothing to say to them that they had not heard many times before. This issue has a long history in Buddhism, and vegetarianism is discussed extensively in many texts in the Buddhist canon. But I reflected that it is not enough that the Buddha and the great lamas have said it. People will not make lasting changes if the reason is just because the Buddha said to do so. If you are doing something because you feel pushed by a person of authority, then when they are not around, you are likely to fall back into your old habits. (I have written more in chapter 8, "Food Justice," about how to hold to our decision to become vegetarian, once we have made the commitment.)

The soundness of the ideas themselves is not enough, either. It is curious—people often think that ideas are more stable than emotions, but if you have no real feeling for an issue, your commitment to it will often be quite unstable. So when I was presenting the issue to the public, I took the arguments that the monks and nuns knew already from the texts, and spoke of them in as immediate and vivid a way as I could.

My basic point was that the best way to protect life was to give up meat. Being vegetarian is a supreme act of saving lives, I reminded them. But I spoke very directly, and made a heartfelt appeal. Then I offered them plenty of options. If they were eating meat several times a day, they might stop for one meal a day or for one day a week, or they might stop completely for the rest of their lives. Then I asked people to consider taking a vow to stop for any time period that suited them.

To my great surprise, between 60 and 70 percent of those listening took a vow that from that day onward, they would stop eating meat of any kind. Some of those who did so were old Tibetan lamas with a long lifetime of eating meat. I have met them since, and they have told me that they were moved to break the habit then and there, once and for all. Word of this talk—and I think maybe also a recording of it—reached Tibet. After that, we heard that meat sales dropped noticeably in the area around Lhasa, the capital of Tibet. The word also spread to my monasteries and even into the villages. Since then, many monks, nuns, and laypeople have stopped eating the meat that was always considered integral to the Tibetan diet.

I really had no expectations that my talk would bring such results. I feel convinced it did so because it was a truly heartfelt appeal. I had no fresh information to offer, but I offered the freshness of my own feelings, and tried to make those feelings come alive for the people listening. This might be one small example of how speaking from the heart can affect others more than ideas alone do.

A Sustainable Relationship to the Planet

We have already seen that our current patterns of consumption of the planet's resources are not sustainable. We are literally in the midst of an environmental crisis. To respond to this crisis, we can examine how and what we consume. Reducing or ending our meat consumption would have an impact, and it is something you can determine to do right now, if you have the wish. We could also be much more creative than we have been thus far in how we apply our human ingenuity in order to produce—and learn to value—material goods that are more durable and less harmful to the environment.

But simply being smarter about how we use our natural resources is not enough to bring about complete environmental sustainability. We need to make our relationship to the environment itself sustainable.

To start with, we can ask ourselves who really owns the planet. We humans like to think that we do. "This land is my land," we say, and kick others off "our" land. But who was here before us? Animals were here before any human beings were, and they are still far more numerous today. We humans are only one of over a million and a half species on this planet. Maybe the animals have a better claim to being the real owners of the planet. What makes us so sure that we should be in charge of it?

Even if it were true that we owned the world, then we should also live up to the responsibility that ownership implies. Actually, if we analyze our situation carefully, we will recognize that we cannot be owners. At best, we can only be guardians, holding the planet in trust for future generations of all kinds of living beings.

We human beings have the capacity to be wise and compassionate guardians of the planet. Humanity is characterized by an ability to distinguish between what is wholesome and what is not, and to hold ourselves accountable for adopting what is beneficial, and eschewing what is harmful. In other words, we have a unique ability to create and live by moral systems. Our human intelligence equips us to identify what brings happiness and what brings suffering. We have the ability to determine what is wholesome for the world and conducive to its health, and what damages it. We can also discern what is wholesome for animals and conducive to their happiness, and what causes them pain.

Given this capacity, it is tragic that we put our intelligence to distorted uses. Right now, we are using up our environment, and using it in the most abusive ways possible. We wantonly toss out consumer goods that still work perfectly well, just to upgrade to something newer, without a thought for the resources consumed or for where the discarded goods will go. We kill animals for food, or even just for fun. Considering all that we take from the earth and those who live on it, what have we given back?

We could actually offer back a great deal, if we were moved to apply our human intelligence and ingenuity to the task of caring for the planet, instead of just taking from it. I believe we need to begin by wedding our intelligence to our emotions, especially the emotion of compassion. We also need ethics as a guide in applying our intelligence. We can bring these three together—intelligence, emotions, and ethics—to consider what is good for all sentient beings, what is good for the environment, and what is good for future generations of human beings. In other words, we can apply our moral systems more widely, so that they are fully inclusive.

Our concern for right and wrong, or benefit and harm, must encompass the animals we share this planet with, as well as the physical environment that hosts us all alike. Using less and using goods that last longer, while very important, in itself will not resolve the situation we now find ourselves in. What can be truly lasting is the healthy application of our attitude of caring and our ability to discern—the engagement of our heart and mind, together. This would form the foundation of a sustainable relationship with the environment.

Material things are limited, but there is no limit to the number of people and animals who will depend on this planet in future generations. They will all be relying on us to leave them a home that can support them. The human qualities of intelligence and compassion are powerful. If we learn to apply these two qualities now to protect the environment, we can actively care for the vast number of beings of the future who are counting on us.

When we base our relationship to the environment in compassion and wisdom, it can become truly sustainable. As human beings, we have the capacity to create such a relationship. If we put our hearts and minds to the task, we can accomplish truly great aims.

8 • Food Justice

Healing the Cycles of Hunger
and Harm

FOOD IS AN AREA OF OUR LIFE where we can directly
experience the kindness we receive from others. It is also an
area where we can perceive our dependence on the planet and on
society.

Every time we sit down to enjoy a meal, we are accepting a gift
from the planet and the people that together provide our sustenance. Every time we eat, we taste our dependence on many other
beings and on the earth itself. Every meal offers a taste of their
kindness to us.

Food brings home all we have discussed of the earth's great
generosity, as well as our intimate connectedness to the world
around us. Each meal we eat arrives on our plate through long,
complex networks involving many people, many plants, and many
animals. The clouds and the soil also join in, and in fact the whole
planet contributes to create the food that we need to survive. Far-
reaching chains of interactions form systems that make our food
available to us, meal after meal, our whole life long.

Unfortunately, many of those systems involve exploitation of
human beings, animals, and the environment. Whether or not we
are aware of this exploitation, we are eating the by-products of it.
We benefit from that exploitation, therefore we bear responsibility

for the tremendous suffering caused to animals in the creation of our food. We bear responsibility for the physical and mental suffering caused to human beings who are working in exploitative conditions in fields or factories, and we bear responsibility, too, for the lasting harm being done to the land and water through the use of fertilizers and pesticides. What's more, many of our food systems have resulted in bringing us food that is harmful to our health.

As grave as all these flaws in the food systems are, the most serious is that they are failing to deliver food to vast numbers of the world's population. Even in the twenty-first century, we still live in a world where far too many people suffer from malnutrition and starvation.

In other words, the food systems supposedly designed to nourish us are instead either harming our bodies, as well as other beings and the planet, or leaving many of us malnourished altogether. When we reach such a point, I think it is high time that we rethink what we are eating and how we as a society produce and distribute our food.

Easier to Change than to Stay the Same

Whether we are talking about social reform to bring about food justice or about spiritual practice, in both cases the starting point is recognizing that we need to make changes. Getting to that point is often the hardest part. Once there, people have different responses. Both social reform and spiritual practice imply modifying our attitudes and our behavior. The prospect of having to make such changes can appear daunting, especially if deep down we suspect that real change is not possible. We can become discouraged before we really begin, feeling that such a shift amounts to having to change our very nature. If we believe that revamping the way our food is produced—and even what we choose to eat—is tantamount to asking a tiger to get rid of its stripes, then the challenge to bring about change will indeed seem insurmountable.

Changing our food systems may initially seem difficult because food is connected to so many aspects of our society and personal life—economics, public policy, social norms, the environment, and our own personal habits. Yet what and how we eat is actually changing all the time. The meat industry has not always been the way it is today. Less than a century ago, there was no McDonald's. Just a few decades ago, there were no chemical fertilizers. A few years ago, there was no such thing as a genetically modified seed. These are all recent innovations.

Moreover, our food systems were created by human interventions, and therefore humans can change them. In fact, our food systems are already in the process of rapid change. They are in a constant state of change. This is just the nature of all things. Indeed, it is harder for systems to remain the same than it is for them to continue changing. What we need to ask ourselves is: In what direction do we want the changes to lead us? As we have seen, to bring about lasting social change, we begin first with an awareness of the necessity for change, and next develop a vision of what positive change would look like. We then have to be moved deeply enough by the issue to act, and finally we will need to root our ongoing actions in a motivation that can sustain them for the long run, until real changes are put in place.

Change in our food systems has to come from us, the individuals who make up society. As I mentioned earlier, society or community is nothing apart from the individuals who comprise it. Therefore, the impetus to make positive changes has to come from individuals—from us. After all, we are the ones ordering, paying for, and eating all the food.

It is up to each of us to identify the specific changes that would make a difference within our own particular food systems. Although some multinational food corporations seem to be everywhere, the food that people eat and the ways that food is produced vary a great deal from one culture and region to another. The food we eat is very much linked to local conditions. My own firsthand knowledge is limited to food systems where I live in India, so I am not in a good position to suggest specific measures for changing how food is produced and distributed in other places. That has to come from each of you, wherever you live—and eat.

The Mirror of the Mind

Even if we accept in principle that we need to make changes in our own personal eating and shopping habits, we tend to want everyone and everything else to change first. There is a story that reminds us how crucial it is that we take responsibility for what we ourselves contribute to the problem, rather than laying all the blame for our harmful food systems on others—or waiting for someone else to fix the problem.

This story tells of a king of a small, remote kingdom in ancient Tibet. In this kingdom, mirrors were extremely rare—practically unheard of. Yet somehow the king managed to acquire a hand mirror, and picked it up one day as he was talking to his faithful old servant. The king took a good look at himself in that mirror, and was not pleased by what he saw. It seems this king was a singularly unattractive man. He felt thoroughly disgusted by the face staring back at him from his mirror. He tossed the mirror aside and exclaimed, "Who is that ugly man? I don't ever want to see him again! Banish this mirror from my kingdom!"

The servant could not keep silent at this. After all the years he had spent gazing on the king's unattractive face, he seized this opportunity to say: "My Lord, I have had to look at you all these years. I do not have the option of just banishing the mirror!"

Like the king in this story, we seem to have a tendency to look at others, but not want to see ourselves. There is a saying in Tibetan: "To see others, you need a pair of eyes. To see yourself, you need the mirror of your own mind."

Recognizing what we are doing to ourselves, to others, and to the world when we eat, is the first step in changing our food systems. Lasting and significant change will not happen by imposing our views on others, or because others impose their views on us. It starts to happen when we look in our mental mirror, and observe that there are positive changes to be made, right here where we are, including the food we choose to consume every day.

In chapter 5, "Consumerism and Greed," I discussed the futility of building our society and our lives on the pursuit of material wealth; the pursuit is by definition endless, because there is no measure of how much is enough. But when it comes to food, there is a clear measure of who does or does not have enough. Malnutrition and starvation are indisputable standards for "not enough." We and the millions of people who go hungry each day are all fellow members of the same global society. We are linked by the same broad food systems. Those of us who are favored by those systems and thus have enough food to eat must consider our responsibility for those who do not.

There is no single, large-scale solution to the problem of world hunger. Nevertheless, the situation was created by many small factors coming together, and so it can also be shifted by many small efforts coming together.

Where Hunger Comes From

Food systems produce not only food, but also hunger. Like other systems—such as education or health-care systems—our food systems tend to benefit the rich. Food systems are linked to our economic systems, and our economic systems themselves favor the rich over the poor. They enable those with more to benefit from the work of those with less.

The rich may say that the reason poor people do not have enough is because they are irresponsible and lazy. I think the finger should be pointing in the other direction. The underlying reason for their poverty is that the poor have been marginalized. We have confined them to their poverty for our own benefit.

And food is a major area where we are benefiting from the exploitation of the poor—poor immigrants who work under the sun in the fields all day, and poor factory workers who process food under exploitative conditions, yet hardly earn enough to feed their families.

Given the technological advances of our era, on the face of things, it is very hard to understand why there is still so much hunger in the world. The cost of one meal eaten by a very rich person could feed a poor person for many days. Earlier, in chapter 6, "Social Action," we were discussing what it really means to be an advanced society. Perhaps indulgence and greed should be signs of lagging behind. Perhaps a willingness to profit at others' expense should be a decisive sign of being "backward."

To say that someone is poor is not quite right; it would be better to say that we have impoverished them. This is the dark side of the "American dream." We blame the poor, accusing them of being poor because they do not work hard enough. Yet for the most part, the poor have less because the rich have taken more. First the poor are overworked and paid barely enough to cover the cost of living. This leaves them unable to pay for higher education that would allow them or their children to advance to better paying professions. Many poor are uninsured, so if anyone in the family faces health issues, they may carry the burden of those medical bills to the end of their days. In this way, our social and economic systems actively confine the poor to their poverty. And after that, we have the audacity to call them backward and lazy!

These dynamics are important to keep in mind so that when we see a hungry person, we do not feel disconnected from their painful lack of food. If we remember that we who have plenty to eat are playing an integral role in their hunger, we can more easily recognize our participation in their suffering, and more readily accept the responsibility to relieve it.

You can begin to make an impact by training yourself to treat your wealth as a conscious responsibility. When you have a full plate, and especially when you have more food than you actually need, you can take that as a reminder that you share the world with those who have less. You can remember that the same systems that produced your food produce their hunger. Developing this habit of remembering their situation will encourage you to seek opportunities to share their suffering and relieve their hunger. In a simple way, each time you have more food than you need, you can become aware that it could feed someone else who does need it. When you learn to feel this deeply, you will be moved to act. That is a great first step.

Rethinking Meat

As we seek ways to make a personal difference with our food consumption, eating meat offers us a valuable lesson and an opportunity. As I discussed in chapter 7, "Environmental Protection," our current level of meat consumption has many detrimental effects on the planet. But if we are thinking in terms of ending world hunger, what should interest us greatly is how many more people we could feed with existing resources if we made a significant shift from meat eating to vegetarianism. Even when animals are crowded into small quarters to save space, the land required to raise their feed is far greater than the land needed to raise vegetarian food of an equivalent nutritional value. As I mentioned earlier, studies show that a single acre of land could feed one meat-eater or twenty vegetarians. This tells us that if our world became vegetarian, we could feed twenty times more people than we now do. If we are serious about ending world hunger, I think this fact deserves very serious attention.

Using our planet's resources to raise animals for slaughter dramatically diminishes the resources that we could more effectively use to feed more people. Is meat eating even sustainable in the long run, if our aim is to end world hunger? I think this is a question we need to ask ourselves.

Whether or not we agree that meat consumption is unsustainable in the long run, I think we can agree that it is not our wisest choice. And it is certainly not our most compassionate choice, either.

If You Are What You Eat . . .

In chapter 7, "Environmental Protection," I encouraged you to consider giving up meat as a step to protect the environment. As you can see, becoming vegetarian is also a way to contribute greatly toward food justice. Some of you may feel that all these arguments are theoretically compelling, but impractical to apply. You may think, "I see the point, but personally I find it difficult to make this step." Or you may have tried to give up meat, but found it hard to keep up your commitment after a while. In this chapter, I would like to offer you all the support I can. To that end, I have a few thoughts to share with you that I hope will sustain you in your decision to reduce your consumption of meat.

You can bear in mind the benefits that you yourself receive. Not only does the meat industry hurt the environment and the animals themselves, but our society's "normal" levels of meat consumption hurt the human body, too. Many people expend a great deal of energy trying to stay healthy. People in the United States and other countries spend countless hours exercising, going to the gym, taking yoga classes, and so on. Yet how is it healthy to eat meat? When you eat meat, you are eating everything that went into the animal. You are eating their growth hormones and antibiotics and vaccinations. You are eating a lifetime of pesticides, since the feed given to animals raised for mass slaughter is hardly likely to be "certified organic"!

This is unhealthy enough to begin with, even before you consider the impact of the way animals are killed. We know a lot about the physical effects of adrenaline, stress, and fear, and we can imagine the sheer terror and panic in the slaughterhouse as animals smell the blood of those who were killed before them. When you eat meat, you ingest not only the chemical substances that animals are full of, but also the emotional and physical stress that animals experience throughout their lives and at the moment of their slaughter. That stress is also part of your meat.

People who have tasted the yogurt in both China and Tibet often comment that the yogurt in Tibet is much tastier. The difference is that Tibetan cows roam freely. When animals are relaxed and happy, the milk and yogurt tastes better. What do milk and meat taste like when they come from animals who were tormented?

Some people may tell you that you must eat meat for your health, for the protein. But this simply is not true. The millions of healthy vegetarians around the world are proof of that fact. Protein sources abound in legumes and other foods that are better for our body and for the environment. It really is just a matter of where we decide to get our protein. I think it is important to recognize that this is a choice we make every time we eat.

Freedom in Eating

It is true that our cultural environment can affect our eating habits. Yet we have the freedom to decide to change. We have complete freedom to eat meat or not. Tibetans live on an arid plateau where herding livestock and eating meat have been central to our culture for millennia. If Tibetans can stop eating meat, so can anyone who lives in a place where vegetables and alternate sources of protein are readily available.

If you need more support against the pressures to eat meat, you could list the reasons why you should not eat meat, and then compare them to the reasons in favor of eating meat. The reasons individuals eat meat are mainly habit and the desire for pleasure. I am sure you will see that the reasons not to eat meat far outweigh such superficial, short-term reasons. The reasons to be vegetarian are realistic and sensible, and based on long-term thinking. When we think seriously about the impact our food practices have on our body, on the environment, and on the animals themselves, it is clear that logic supports abstaining from eating meat.

If you decide you want to try to stop eating meat, you can fortify yourself in this way with reason. Empower your mind, and take responsibility for your body. Exercise your wisdom, strengthen your resolve, and let your mind take good care of your body.

The Choice Is Yours

No one can compel you to eat meat or to be vegetarian. You have to think carefully for yourself, and then act according to your own values and for your own reasons. There is a story about a Chinese emperor who wanted to support vegetarianism. He banned meat eating, and made it punishable by a heavy penalty. Within this empire there was a man whose wife caught him eating meat once, and reported him to the authorities. Clearly, avoiding legal trouble is not the right motivation for becoming vegetarian! The reasons have to be compelling and convincing enough to change our mental attitudes, not just our physical actions. Only a change in attitude can sustain changes in our behavior in the long run.

This choice simply cannot be foisted on us from outside. We see the reality of what happens to the animals. But all the information in the world is not enough if our heart is not moved. We need to make a decision from the depths of our heart, so that we just do not want meat, and so that this feeling is genuine and arises spontaneously.

The good thing is, if you give up meat for a while and then slip back, you can always try again. There is no reason why you cannot make a new effort. It will not be a loss to try again and again.

Finally, if you want to give up meat, but can't seem to get rid of the habit, one solution is to put yourself in the cage where the animals are held before slaughter. Spend some time in there. If you like chicken, spend some time in a chicken coop. If you like pork, spend time in a sty, if only in your imagination. See how it feels. Then decide.

Intentional Eating

Whatever you decide, eating or not eating meat is a choice, and it is best to make it consciously. If you choose to eat meat, you should acknowledge that it is an option you are choosing, and that it is not the only option open to you.

We ate meat in Tibet mainly due to the isolated location and arid climate. But because we are a Buddhist culture, when we ate meat, we knew that we were doing something not quite right. We did not simply feel entitled to kill and consume animals at will. We had some moral compunction about eating the bodies of other sentient beings, and we ate accordingly.

There is a saying in Tibetan that sounds contradictory: "Eat meat with compassion." This does not mean we seek out meat to eat because we are compassionate, but rather that if we find ourselves in a situation where we are eating meat, we do so with full compassion for the animal we are eating. We recite prayers for them. We express our gratitude to the animal. In this way, Tibet developed a culture of eating meat with compassion for the animal who died for our sustenance.

Let me share with you a tale that may seem shocking, but offers a powerful image of eating meat with compassion. The story is set long ago, in a rich and fertile region that typically enjoyed bountiful harvests. At a certain point, the region was struck by a severe and prolonged drought. At the time, an older couple was living with their adult son. The family had been accustomed to eating well, but wisely began to limit their consumption. But even after strictly rationing their food stores, eventually it all ran out, and one day the three of them were left with absolutely nothing to eat.

As they faced starvation together, the parents told their son, "If we die, then you must survive on us. You must eat our flesh."

"Absolutely not!" the son said. "You must survive on me. I will be watching from beyond to be sure that you do. You must not let my flesh go to waste."

That night, the son killed himself in order to keep his parents alive. He did this to offer his body to them with great love and compassion. Recalling his words, the grief-stricken parents forced themselves to eat the meat from his body, with great reluctance and terrible sadness for the loss of their child. With each bite, they experienced an unbearable sense of indebtedness to their son and his sacrifice.

If you do eat meat, this story offers a model of the attitude to have when you are eating an animal's flesh. Please do not mistake the point of this story. The point is not to condone suicide—far from it. It is not meant to equate cannibalism with meat eating, either. Rather, the point is to recognize that meat is something we receive at the cost of the life of another being. Although the animals we eat did not have the option of giving their lives voluntarily as the son in this story did, nevertheless they did lose what was most precious to them in the world—their lives—so that some people could enjoy meat in their dishes. We ought to acknowledge the animals' sacrifice when we are eating their meat, not wolfing it down unthinkingly, and certainly not wasting it by throwing it out uneaten.

Two Obstacles: Desire and Habit

As I mentioned earlier, I used to eat a lot of meat when I lived in Tibet. There was dry meat from the area around my monastery in Tibet that I really liked. I was not alone in liking it. That meat from the area around Tsurphu Monastery was so famous that politicians used to come from Lhasa asking for it. I can still remember the taste of that dried Tsurphu meat, which I ate just for the flavor. It was a matter of habit. But by blindly following that habit as a child, I became attached to the taste. Even now, though I have been vegetarian for years, there are times I miss the flavor of that dried meat.

As in my case, many of our eating patterns originate in sheer, mindless habit. We crave what we grew up eating. This is just a matter of what we have cultivated a taste for. We can definitely cultivate a new taste for healthy foods. In other words, we can cultivate healthier desires.

Buddhist texts speak of three different types of desire—positive desires, negative desires, and desires that are mixed. Positive desires are defined as desires for things that are good for you. Negative desires are desires for things that harm you. Mixed desires combine both harm and benefit. If you are going to let your eating choices be driven by desire, it is important to develop desires that are positive and healthy. This is possible to do, but only if your desires are guided by your wisdom and not by your attachment. The principle telling you what you want should be reason. When negative desires arise, you should recognize them as harmful and stop chasing after them.

This process requires you to remain attentive and fully aware of what you are doing. You can avoid falling into harmful eating habits in much the same way you would avoid obstacles when driving your car. You remain alert when you drive, so that when you see a potential danger in your path, you steer the car in another direction. Don't let unhealthy habits and desires damage your vehicle. Steer yourself away as soon as you see them coming. You can use this as a way to wean yourself off old eating patterns, and develop new and healthier tastes.

When Food Is Toxic

When we look at the selection on the average supermarket shelf, it becomes clear how important it is that we start making conscious choices, guided by wisdom rather than desire and habit. Over the past decades, we humans have applied our ingenuity to inventing new ways to produce food. Pesticides, genetically modified seeds, and new processing methods combine to make food easier and more profitable to grow or raise. Yet at the same time, these very foods seem to be increasingly poisonous to the environment and to the very bodies they are supposed to nourish.

What can we do about this? We obviously cannot stop eating. As we understand more about how our food is produced and what it contains, we may not want to buy anything at all. It might seem that "progress" in food production is making things worse. We may even dream of going back to the days before supermarkets and fast food, and just grow all our own food. Although this could be a worthy endeavor, it is simply not practical in most cases. Even if we could begin to grow some herbs or a few vegetables, most of us will basically remain consumers and not major producers of food. Therefore, as consumers we must make the best possible choices among what is available right now, and work to see that there are better choices available for all in the future.

For example, you may not be able to afford to buy only organic products. Even if you can afford to eat purely organic, you might not find everything available where you live. Or organic foods might be sold but not grown in your area. Flying in or trucking in food from faraway regions consumes a lot of fossil fuels, and so eating food that was not grown locally has other adverse impacts on the environment. For many reasons, the ideal option in terms of health and environmental impact may simply not be available to you. But as long as you are aware of what you are eating, you will at least make better choices within what is possible in your individual circumstances. By contrast, if you remain unaware or refuse to consider these issues, you cannot help but cause some form of harm—to your own body, to the environment, or to the people and animals exploited in order to produce your food.

A Practice for the Supermarket

You can consciously work on becoming a more enlightened participant in these food systems. One simple practice you could adopt is to pause briefly at the entrance to the supermarket, or wherever you shop for food.

Just take a moment to adjust your attitude. Instead of the usual approach—that you have come there to make purchases—tell yourself that you have come to make choices. Make the aspiration that your choices will make a difference for others. As you enter the store, envision that you are treading the same path as many other people who are similarly seeking to make wise choices. Then, as you walk through the store, keep in mind that the choices you are making form a crucial component of the food systems that deliver food to everyone in your society. What you see available on the shelves reflects what people have been choosing to buy. Every purchase you make will support certain food industries, and send a small signal of approval and acceptance.

While you are shopping, you can think of the kind of food options you would like everyone to have available to them, and put those items in your cart. You can think of the kinds of food industries or practices you want to see changed, and keep their items out of your cart. As you do this, you can hold in your heart a hope that the choice you make today will join with the choices of other like-minded shoppers to bring lasting changes that will benefit many others, too.

If you approach food shopping in this spirit, you will naturally want to take some initiatives to better inform your choices. There is already a great deal of information available about commercial food products. It would be great if someone would create a phone app that would help us access and analyze all the relevant information about each item on the supermarket shelves. Along with the list of ingredients, we need information about where each item comes from, how far it traveled, its impact on our health, how it was grown or slaughtered or manufactured, and how the company treats its workers. When you are standing in the supermarket, you could use this information to identify products that cause less suffering to your body, to animals, to humans, and to the environment.

It is up to us to educate ourselves not just on general issues of nutrition, but about the particular food items we are eating. This would allow us to better understand and anticipate the immediate and long-term consequences of our food practices. Actively seeking out and using sources of information about food products gives us alternatives and options. It can also send a clear message to big companies that we are aware of what they are doing, and ready to act on our awareness.

The fact that today there are vegetarian restaurants in many cities, and vegetarian options in many nonvegetarian restaurants, is visible proof that the food choices we make as individuals have the collective power to bring about change. After enough individuals inquired about vegetarian options, restaurant managers recognized that it was in their interest to add vegetarian selections to their menus. The same happened with organic foods in supermarkets. We should not underestimate our power to bring about change.

The Danger of the Easy Way Out

Today's food systems have yielded a great variety of food options. This offers us some advantages, including the availability of alternative sources of protein to meat. However, much of what is newly available is sold not because it is more nutritious and compassionate, but because it is more convenient and tasty. We have already noted the importance of managing our desires for certain tastes. If we are to make better personal choices about what to eat and what food systems to support, we must also be careful not to let ourselves be taken in by the lure of ease and accessibility.

We are constantly busy, and live chasing the clock as if we were machines. But machines never need to eat or take a break. Our machine mentality leads us to value efficiency and productivity. This has caused us great damage in terms of the food systems we have developed, and also in our own attitudes toward the food we eat.

There is a story about a great meditator who was led astray by taking the easy way out. This is said to have taken place at a time when many Tibetans were given immigrant visas to the United States. Among them was a highly accomplished meditator. His English skills were no better than most other Tibetans, he had no professional expertise, and he was considered fortunate to find an extremely easy job that paid fairly well. He had no clear idea what this company did as a whole, but it seemed like an ideal job for someone like him with no marketable skills. All he had to do was sit quietly in front of a machine and push some buttons.

He spent his hours at work saying his prayers, meditating on universal compassion, and pushing that button every so often as he had been trained to do. Sometime later, one of his cousins visited him at work, curious to see what this easy job was. The visitor was more inquisitive than his cousin, and discovered that the machine killed chickens. The meditator was monitoring the machine, and when everything was lined up to kill the chickens, a signal came, and he pushed some buttons and pulled some levers that operated a machine that effected the slaughter out of his sight.

When the meditator realized what he had been doing, he was horrified. He was overcome with such remorse that he handed back his paycheck. The boss thought he was crazy. The meditator quit this murderous job, and later it seems he went into retreat.

We often fail to see what is actually going on around us, or the broader systems and institutions that we are a part of. We follow along, and do not see our role in the larger food systems. If we are comfortable in our own little corner, like this meditator, we do not even ask ourselves what the system as a whole is creating or destroying. This can have devastating consequences, not just for us now, but for the future as well.

There is nothing inherently wrong with things being easy or convenient. The problems come when we make ease the most important criterion when considering what and how to eat. When we take a long-term perspective, what is easy and convenient often looks like a foolish and shortsighted basis for our decisions.

Think of today's children, of future generations. What are we passing on to them? For many centuries, human beings have handed down their wisdom and experience to subsequent generations. Old ways and wisdom were valued and passed on, because they were found to be thoughtful, sensible, and beneficial. They had stood the test of time.

Knowing how to cook is one example of this. This skill is rapidly becoming one of the "old ways"—something people used to do in olden times. (Though perhaps I should not talk, because I myself do not know how to cook!) Learning to cook even just one dish from scratch is a simple but significant step we can take. Cooking could be a way to bring people together, and bring warmth, closeness, and health into the home and into our family or community of friends.

The Greatness of Small Acts

Bringing about food wisdom in our own life and bringing about food justice in the world are long-term aims, vast in scope. We must not allow ourselves to become discouraged thinking of the big things we cannot accomplish all at once. We should not discount small acts because they do not eliminate world hunger in one fell swoop.

Small acts can be huge. Our very existence on this planet depends on small acts. Countless small acts have joined together to sustain our life. Numberless seeds have been planted, and numberless hands have quietly nurtured the plants. Each seed is tiny and each hand may be quite small, but together they yield the vast harvests that fuel all human activity on this planet.

We each depend on the presence of countless causes and conditions for our life to be possible. This same principle of interdependence means that our presence is also a condition for others' well-being and happiness. Our life takes place in a context of complete and constant interconnectedness. This means that everything we do can have some impact on others. This principle is how we developed large-scale food systems in the first place.

When it gets cold where I live in northern India, I often wrap myself in a blanket or drape it over my knees. As I do, I recall the people in the much poorer area of Bodh Gaya who have nothing. There are many who live in the streets there, with only their begging bowl to their name. When I hold my blankets, I think of them. I make aspirations and prayers that they may have blankets as well, and I make a firm determination that the next time I visit Bodh Gaya, I will bring blankets for them. Similarly when we eat, we can also think about how to share our food with the hungry in small but direct ways. Clearly, one blanket or meal will not eliminate their poverty or end world hunger. But it fosters an attitude that can bring results in the long run.

When you truly root yourself in a sense of responsibility and caring, then you will naturally act to ease the pain you see. Instead of being idealistic or waiting for the chance to have a big impact, you will be moved to act in small ways. And in the long run, this sense of deep concern will sustain your movements far beyond one single act.

Even in the short term, making a practical difference in just one person's life is highly worthwhile. Ending the pain of an individual who is suffering is deeply meaningful. If you can make a difference in a few people's lives, that is something major. The most important thing is to be sincere, and to remain sincerely conscientious about the responsibility that comes with the food you eat.

Then, you just have to start somewhere. You can stop eating

meat. You can donate a certain percentage of what you earn to worthy causes. Educate yourself. Set an example for your peers. Open your heart. Share and give. Inspire others to do the same. This is how big things start.

9 • Conflict Resolution
Anger Is the Problem

W E ALL DEPEND ON one another. For this reason, whenever we act according to self-interest, sooner or later our selfish aims are bound to clash with the aims of the people we rely upon to accomplish our own goals. When that happens, conflicts will inevitably arise. As we learn to be more balanced in valuing others' concerns with our own, we will naturally find ourselves involved in fewer and fewer conflicts. In the meantime, it is helpful to acknowledge that conflicts are the logical outcome of this combination of self-interest and interdependence. Once we recognize this, we can see that conflicts are nothing to feel shocked or offended by. Rather, we can address them calmly and with wisdom.

The same principle of interdependence that brings us into conflict with others when we act selfishly can also bring us into harmony when we take others' well-being into consideration. Interdependence also makes it possible for a sincerely concerned third party to intervene and help resolve others' conflicts. In this chapter, I would like to explore ways to end conflicts that we ourselves are involved in, as well as conflicts between other parties.

There are many different kinds of conflict, but the worst ones are those fueled by anger. Conflict per se is not necessarily harmful, but whenever anger is present, harm of some sort is done. This is because, at a minimum, any time anger arises it is disturbing to the person who is angered. If we are committed to working to defuse conflicts, it is important to understand this destructive force that drives so many of them.

Conflicts Fueled by Anger

Anger arises out of a disgruntled, unhappy state of mind. Once anger is present, it feeds on unhappiness and mental agitation. We can see from direct experience that upsetting and disturbing others just causes their anger to increase. We need to be aware that when we upset others, we create a condition for their anger to arise or escalate. This is a terrible way to treat another person.

Anger inflicts serious harm on all those around the angry person. A whole family, a community, and even society at large can all be affected by the presence of anger within it. People may respond to others' anger with fear, or they may become agitated and angry themselves. Increasing levels of hostility within a community bring increasing stress, conflict, and even violence. For this reason, it is crucial that we ourselves are free of aggression and anger when we try to end the conflicts that we are part of, as well as when we intervene in others' problems. If we bring our own anger to the conflict, we will end up fueling it further.

We can all see that when people are angry, they are more liable to harm the person at whom their anger is directed. But it is very important also to see that anger hurts the person who is angry. Here is how that works. First we believe that someone has wronged us in some way. We find this completely unacceptable. Once anger sets in, we become convinced that we are absolutely right to feel resentment. We want the other person to get what we are sure they deserve. Our mood is dark, and we churn with this anger. Unpleasant as this state is, we actively nurture it, looking for more wrongs they have done in order to feed our anger. We do not want to hear anything good about the person. We get more and more caught up in thoughts of vengeance and other negative thoughts. We quickly reach the point where we lose our appetite and can hardly sleep at night. Even before we have approached the person we want to harm, we have already harmed ourselves a great deal. This is truly foolish.

Anger further harms us by clouding our judgment. We cannot think or act effectively if we are overcome with anger. We do not want to see the positive side of the person—and that is the side we urgently need to connect with in order to resolve the situation. Our anger blinds us, and we are more interested in plotting revenge than in resolving the conflict amicably.

There is an example of an old woman in ancient Tibet who became furious at the rulers of the country. For three years, she fumed and stewed in her hatred for the government. But they hardly even knew she existed. They certainly were unaware of her anger toward them. She was just causing herself misery and pain. All that anger harmed only her. What a tremendous loss for her.

Slowly Poisoning Ourselves

Much of our anger is just like this old woman's. Anger causes suffering. It is toxic. When we harbor resentment and anger, we are willingly ingesting poison. Because we do not recognize this, we keep eating what is toxic to our system, and only take note when the effects of the poisoning have become so painfully obvious that we can no longer deny them.

For example, let's imagine a man who has an argument with a family member at home in the morning. He leaves for work, but he stops on his way to get a cup of coffee at a Starbucks. He is so agitated that he fumbles the coffee and it spills on his suit. He gets even more upset. Then, traffic is moving too slowly for him. He shouts and pounds the steering wheel. He takes his frustration out on the accelerator and gets into a fender bender. Now he is really furious. When he gets into the elevator at work, he is like a caged animal ready to lash out at anyone who comes near. He scowls at the other people in the elevator. When he reaches the office, his boss says, "Hey, you're late." This small comment becomes the last straw. He snaps at his boss, saying, "Why are you always getting on my case? Who do you think you are, anyway?" He throws down his briefcase and storms out.

In this way, a small argument in the morning has ended up causing this man the loss of his job. A few days later when he sits at home unemployed, he might rightly wonder how on earth things went so wrong so quickly.

This is just a story, but we might recognize some of ourselves in it. We all encounter situations that could upset us, but we do not need to engage so fully with them. This man gave himself over, 100 percent, to each little thing that disturbed him. He had nothing left to anchor him, and so he was thrown completely off balance. Instead, even if we feel some sense of disturbance at situations that occur, we should not completely plunge into them. We have the option of staying grounded within ourselves. Even when we are in the middle of disturbing situations, we need to hold the larger percentage of ourselves back from them. We need to hold to our own center.

I think it is fair to say that anger is a form of illness that affects our mind—a certain kind of mental illness! We go to the doctor for annual checkups, but we also need to examine our mind for mental afflictions. These can be much more serious than many physical afflictions. When it comes to managing our anger, many of us act like people who think about their health only after they have become ill. We should not wait until the symptoms are manifesting themselves. Again and again, we need to check ourselves for signs of the presence of mental afflictions—including anger. This is the best way to protect our inner health and happiness. When we learn to manage our anger, we will find ourselves involved in fewer and fewer conflicts, and will certainly cause less harm to ourselves and others when conflicts do arise.

Becoming Cause-Oriented

When we look at ourselves honestly, there will surely be times when we recognize that we are contributing to a conflict. We may want to be part of the solution, but we find that we are actually part of the problem.

We often cause conflicts with others and problems for ourselves because we focus on results rather than causes. We want happiness, but we do not pay attention to the causes of happiness. It is clear that anger does not bring happiness, but pain and distress. We have no wish for pain and unhappiness, but we cling to views and conduct that cause them. Instead of trying to be results-oriented, perhaps we need to be more cause-oriented.

It is actually quite simple. When we use our intelligence, we can easily see the relation between causes and results. Since we depend on others to achieve our goals, our intelligence tells us that we cannot expect to accomplish our aims by pitting ourselves against others. Thinking of others and caring about their well-being is a far wiser and more effective way to bring about our own well-being than caring exclusively about our own individual needs. Once we recognize the connections between cause and result, and self and others, we can learn how to direct ourselves toward causes that will bring the results we desire, and away from causes that bring the results we do not want.

Don't plant the seeds of your own suffering. Embrace the conditions for healthier growth. Put simply, if you wish to avoid unhappiness, avoid its causes. Fighting with others brings unhappiness. You may enter into a conflict, thinking it will yield some measure of happiness, but you are just planting innumerable seeds of pain and trouble.

Speaking to Those Who Don't Listen

Conflicts can occur when we encounter people whose ideas are fundamentally opposed to our own. Of course, diversity of opinions does not have to lead to conflict. It all depends on how we relate to the views we hold. For example, some people can be fundamentalist about their own views, and unreceptive to any views that diverge from their own. For this reason, some people can simply be harder to reason with than others.

People in the part of Tibet that I come from are called Khampas, and we Khampas have a reputation for being stubborn and unwilling to listen to others' views. There used to be a saying in Tibetan: "Khampas have their ears on their bottoms," meaning you get us to listen not by speaking to us, but by smacking us. This may be said jokingly, but there is a certain grain of truth in it. Khampa culture often displays a reluctance to open to others' views, as do other cultures, too, of course. We sometimes meet people who seem so deaf to divergent opinions that we may wonder where their ears are—and not only among us Khampas!

When we do encounter people we find to be arrogant or hardheaded, there is a tendency to want to break through their resistance by being forceful with them. Similarly, when faced with someone who is angry, we often feel that we should not be soft or gentle, for fear that they will ignore us or even take our gentleness for weakness and attack us. I think we ought to consider carefully whether this is really the right approach. If you add your own anger to another person's, it just results in more anger—and makes it harder to find a shared way forward together.

As we see, various emotional forces can keep people from listening to views that differ from their own. Stubbornness is one. A temporary upheaval of anger is another. We need to find ways to interact productively with people who are unable or unwilling to broaden their thinking in order to take in others' perspectives.

In such cases, it is up to us to find a healthy way to relate to their vantage point.

Letting Go of Righteousness

If you think about it, we human beings can be really strange. When our views come into conflict with others, we are always sure that our way of seeing things must be right. No matter what position each of us is defending, both sides cling to the same unquestioned conviction that the error must be entirely on the other's side. This is really not rational, is it?

The same is true of our interests. We are always so confident in promoting our own aims, as if what is best for us must automatically be best for the whole world. Every human being has their own individual views and personal goals, but whoever we are, we are absolutely certain that our goals are the most important, and our views are the most reasonable. We get so completely caught up in our intense concern to pursue our own aims that nothing else really seems to make sense to us. This is self-centeredness, pure and simple.

If another person gets in the way of our aims, we are willing to cut them down—even people close to us who have shown us great kindness. It goes against all reason that simply because something is ours, it is best. And even if our aims are best, we need to ask ourselves whether we have the right to pursue them at others' expense.

My own way of thinking about this is that when we are meeting with angry or stubborn people, we should bring even greater understanding to bear. The more closed-minded or hardheaded someone seems, the more reason there is for us to be open-minded and gentle when interacting with them. We can recognize how difficult and painful it is to live with anger or narrow views, and this allows us to feel compassion for them.

I have spoken of anger as a kind of mental affliction. I think the analogy of how we respond to people who are insane might give us a model for reacting with greater kindness to extreme cases of closed-mindedness. When we encounter people who are acting outright crazy, we recognize that they are not in their right minds, and respond accordingly. We do not insist that they see things our way. We do not become angry when we observe their lack of control over their own minds. Rather, we can maintain our equanimity and can see that they are suffering. If they appear to be completely deaf to what we are saying, or shout at us when we speak calmly to them, we take it as an indication of a kind of loss of sanity, and feel even greater compassion toward them. As a result, we are even more concerned and sensitive to their condition.

I believe engaging in the same spirit of compassion could help us relate more productively with people who are clearly sane, but are nevertheless unwilling or unable to listen to our views. We do not need to take it personally, but can regard them with affection and sensitivity.

This is my suggestion: use your understanding. Understanding is crucial in all human communication. When faced with people who are inflexible in their views, that is the time for you to be at your most flexible and accommodating, and to bring all your wisdom and compassion to bear.

Clinging to Problems

When I observe some of our behavior, it really looks to me as if we human beings actually want to suffer. Judging from the way we act, we do not appear to be truly interested in happiness. Instead, it is suffering that we grab with both hands and hold on to. We do not act in ways that can bring about real happiness. It is as if we already had a surplus of happiness, but have a serious shortage of misery and suffering, and so need to actively seek it out. This really is crazy.

In actual reality, we lack true, authentic happiness, but cling instead to what deceptively appears to us as happiness. If we are angry, and someone says something kind and conciliatory to us, we do not even want to hear it. We seem to want to keep the painful experience of anger alive and close, and keep kindness and happiness at bay. We act as if we treasure suffering, so whenever we find it, we don't want to let it go.

It is really just a matter of what we hold on to. In such cases, we are holding on to a certain erroneous self-understanding. We are operating on a mistaken assumption that who we are is only that angry, disturbed person. But we do not have to be that person. There is no single identity that can define us completely. At any moment, we have the option of being different; we can be a person who is not angry or disturbed. Let yourself be that other person—a person who treasures true happiness, kindness, and tranquillity.

You, me, and everyone in the world has experienced various forms of kindness from others again and again throughout our lives. Why don't you hold on to and treasure those experiences? Look carefully at your experiences to recognize all the love you have received. Look carefully at your own actions and gestures to find ways to show love. Make room for that in your heart, and painful conflicts will lose their sting.

Receiving Uninvited Advice

Not all conflict is based on directly opposing interests. Sometimes we come into conflict with people who actually have our interests at heart, but simply have a different understanding than we do of what is best for us. There are certain stages in life and certain situations where we are prone to receive a good deal of uninvited advice. As young adults, we are surrounded by many different people telling us what we should do—parents, aunts, uncles, grandparents, older siblings, teachers, and bosses. We find differences in personal viewpoints as well as generational differences. When the gaps in thinking and age are great, even small comments can end up causing disputes and disharmony.

Whether such disputes arise due to a difference in generations or just due to a basic difference in perspective, the pattern is similar. You do not welcome their advice, and may even try to avoid the other person. You may actively resent the fact that they find fault with your behavior, your lifestyle, or even your personality. You may exaggerate the encounters you have with them, and hold on to the feeling of hurt.

However, it is not in your interest to blame others for resentment that you yourself are harboring. Convincing yourself that this is the only way you could feel or react to the situation does not help you at all. It just keeps you stuck in that unhappy frame of mind, and keeps you viewing others in a dark light.

I would like to share something from my own personal experience. I am not sure how this would work in other contexts, but it helped me move beyond this sort of conflict. I mentioned that since I left home for the monastery when I was seven years old, I have had different caretakers and guardians. One older monk has a tendency to be quite nitpicky, and to constantly correct me on matters I consider completely trivial. This happens a lot, and we live together in close quarters, so I had to develop a way to deal with it. What I came up with was this: Whenever he would start scolding me, I would imagine that he was talking about another person—not about me, but about someone else. Then I would mentally take my caretaker's side in the argument against this third person. I would nod in agreement with my caretaker's criticism, and inwardly say to myself, "Oh yes, what an awful guy that Karmapa is. Look what he did. Can you believe it? How could anyone wear such wrinkled clothes!" It became a game that I could play whenever this caretaker started in on me. It was actually fun, and I got to the point that I quite enjoyed it. Most importantly, it allowed me to keep my feelings of affection and warmth toward this monk alive and strong, no matter what was going on between us. I could remember that he was doing his best to care for me, in his own way.

At certain stages in life and in certain situations, we may also find ourselves in the position of having to care for others in ways that they do not immediately appreciate. For example, as adults we have the responsibility to guide children, and steer them away from destructive behavior or situations. Even as adults, unless we are immediately able to see the wisdom of advice offered to us, we often reject it as intrusive or offensive.

Young children are inquisitive and curious. They are trying to work things out for themselves, so it can be very effective to explain the reasons for the instructions and guidance we give them. Rather than mandating behavior or imposing a discipline based on external authority, it is better to help them see the results of acting in a certain way. The long-term goal is for them to adopt the values as their own, rather than experience them as externally imposed.

When we talk to children, we can try to put sense into their heads, but just as importantly, we should try to put sense into their hearts. We should have the patience to talk to children, to educate them. Teach children how to value their own principles. Our aim should be to instill in them good ways of thinking and feeling for themselves.

Intervening in Others' Disputes

Apart from all the conflicts we ourselves might be involved in, there may be conflicts between other people in our family, circle of friends, or wider community. Once we can ensure that we will bring no anger to bear when facing these conflicts, we can begin to think about helping others to resolve their conflicts. If we see an opportunity to offer constructive advice, I feel that it is important to do so. The best advice goes straight to the heart of a problem, and points out the underlying issues. We know from when we are embroiled in conflicts ourselves that it can be hard to recognize how our own behavior or attitude might be contributing to the problem. Sometimes it just takes another person to zero in on our faults, and reveal them to us.

However, to do this constructively for others requires not only a sincere wish to benefit those involved; it also takes considerable skill. While we begin with noble aspirations, we then need to implement our aspirations with wisdom and discernment. We must take into account the circumstances and the timing. The person in question needs to want to hear what we have to say, and to have a basic willingness to change. When people are willing to change, speaking to them about their faults can be extremely beneficial. But if they do not want to listen or to change, despite our best intentions telling them what we see may just upset them.

When it comes to intervening in others' conflicts, acting on our good intentions without wisdom can be dangerous. If we are not careful, a sense of righteousness can creep in. We may start to feel that our good intentions entitle us to dispense advice or to intervene, whether the circumstances warrant it or not.

Global Conflicts, Global Solutions

Until now, we have been speaking primarily of interpersonal conflicts. Much of what we have noticed in such conflicts can also be seen in conflicts arising on a community or international scale. Conflicts occur not only between individuals, but also between groups of all sizes, including entire nations—and they often occur for similar reasons, and follow patterns similar to those found in conflicts between individuals. For that reason, when bigger and more powerful nations step in to offer guidance to other nations, many of the same principles apply as when individuals intervene to resolve interpersonal conflicts. A sincere motivation is absolutely key, and on top of that, the intervention must be done with sensitivity and skill.

In this small world we live in, nations coexist interdependently. The actions of one country affect others deeply. Countries with more power have the potential to influence others more. I believe that with this power comes a great deal of responsibility, and that includes the responsibility not to exercise one's power over others in pursuit of the private interests of one's own nation.

When it comes to global conflicts, the United States of America has a reputation for being the world's disciplinarian. It is a permanent member of the United Nations Security Council. Of course, built in to that position is a moral responsibility. While I cannot claim to be fully aware of what actually transpires on the ground, it does seem that the world's opinion of America is decidedly mixed.

I myself have warm feelings for the people of the United States. I have had two opportunities to travel abroad since I arrived in India, and both times I went to America. My predecessor, His Holiness the Sixteenth Karmapa, also visited the continent on numerous occasions and passed away in Chicago, which we Tibetans take as a meaningful sign of a special connection to the people of that country. Personally, I myself feel a close connection to America. Yet I do have the impression that it is as famous for the good it does as it is notorious for the bad. There is the view that while the United States does much that is helpful, it also displays a tendency to interfere in other countries' internal affairs. I think there may be some truth to the widely held perception that business and trade dictate what the American government thinks are its country's interests.

While I firmly believe that powerful countries have a responsibility to use their position and resources for the welfare of others, I also think that stepping in to mediate others' conflicts should only be done with a view to benefiting the parties involved, never with a view to furthering one's own interests. From the outside, it does often look as if the major world powers intervene primarily to protect their own interests, commercial or otherwise.

Not all the major world powers grant their citizens a real voice in deciding policy. But when the possibility of intervening is debated publicly, as citizens of powerful democracies you have a responsibility to take an active role in examining the motives for the policies that are made in your name. It would not be wise to uncritically accept the information presented in public reports and the decisions made by your political leaders. You have to look very carefully for any ulterior motives.

This guideline applies when a country steps in to resolve others' conflicts, and also when an individual steps in. You have to be very honest with yourself about the motivation. You need to be sure you are seeing the situation impartially, and not relying on the view from just one side. Before you approve the actions proposed, you should be confident that they are in the best interest not only of your country, but of the world as a whole. To be a responsible, conscious citizen, it is important that you think for yourself, and take universal peace, stability, and well-being into account. Use your discernment and take a stand that serves the whole world, not just one corner of it.

Even when we are sure that the motivation to contribute positively to the well-being of the world is sincere, we also have to scrutinize the means used to pursue that aim. For example, in the name of bringing freedom to other countries, weapons are produced and wars are waged. As powerful countries themselves expand their arsenals and wage more war, the peace and stability of their own country and of the world are both placed at risk.

Again, a pure motivation needs to be applied with wisdom. I feel very strongly that war and fighting are not an effective means to bring about peace or prosperity, stability or freedom. I am certain that history will demonstrate war to be ineffective and counterproductive in the long run.

I have met many people from powerful countries who are deeply unhappy with how their leaders wield their power internationally. This seems especially common when people have failed in their efforts to urge the decision makers to pursue a more compassionate and skillful course. Some of these people become angry at their own governments. In other cases, people direct their anger at the governments of other countries.

If you find yourself angry at any government, please recollect how harmful anger is to yourself and others, and steady yourself with a firm resolve. Make an unwavering commitment to yourself that you will not allow your mind to become perturbed. Be immovable—unshakable from a peaceful state of mind.

Facing Any Challenge

There is a Buddhist saying that can help strengthen your determination to keep your balance in any challenging situation. It says: "If you can do something to change the circumstances, why be upset about it? And if you cannot do anything to change the circumstances, why be upset about it?"

This saying is relevant to all situations in life. If you can do something to improve matters, wonderful. There is no reason to be distressed. On the other hand, there is certainly no point in worrying about something you cannot change. This advice applies when you seek to influence the way your government intervenes in others' conflicts. It also applies when you are attempting to resolve other people's conflicts. It applies when you yourself come into conflict with others.

In fact, this advice covers all circumstances in life. Most situations can be changed, but some cannot. Either way, there is no cause to become agitated or feel unhappy. If you really think about this, then when you allow yourself to become disturbed or unhappy, you really cannot say it is someone else or something else making you upset. It is you causing your own unhappiness. Why let yourself become stuck in an untenable position? In situations where change is possible you work for change; where it is not possible, you accept that fact and work within the bounds of what is possible.

In short, there is no point to being disturbed and unhappy. You only hurt yourself: you do not fix the situation or benefit others. You just make it harder for yourself to access the wholesome resources that you have within your own mind. You just deny yourself access to your own noble heart.

Starting with Ourselves

For all these reasons, when we work to solve conflicts, I think the best place to start is with ourselves. The best advice we give is given to ourselves, not to others. In Buddhist teachings, each person is said to be his or her own protector or "savior." This reminds us that in the end, we each have to direct our own actions, and realize for ourselves which way the wholesome path lies.

If we tend to prefer to give advice to others rather than to ourselves, we may develop a tendency to focus on others' deficiencies, while remaining blind to our own. We may even start to hide our faults from ourselves and from others. Then we will not notice where we need to improve until someone else comes along and forces us to look at our flaws. Waiting for others to criticize us is not a reliable strategy for determining where our problems lie! When we notice a problem and can see for ourselves where it comes from within us, that is when we are most moved to try to fix it.

It also helps to recognize that many conflicts will not be resolved in a single encounter. Some conflicts might not be resolved for a very long time. Yet whether or not you succeed in resolving a conflict that you observe or are yourself involved in, you always have options. Whatever happens, you can work on yourself. In order not to become overwhelmed or disturbed while a conflict is taking place, you can cultivate your own inner qualities. If you can develop your qualities and remain true to your own pure aspirations, at the very least you will always be able to take heart in knowing that there is one less harmful person in the world.

Trust

Once a conflict is resolved, the ongoing work is to rebuild trust. Even after conflicts have ended, we often find it difficult to reestablish open and easy relationships with the opposing party. We may feel bruised by the experience, and our trust can be damaged. Resolving conflicts on any scale—personal, community, or global—is not enough. We also need to cultivate a basis of trust, to support the long-term healing of the relationship between two parties.

In my life, I have had some mixed experiences when it comes to placing my trust in others. On various occasions, the kind of treatment or behavior that I expected from others was not forthcoming, and this has led me to think a good deal about what trust means to me. What I have come to feel is that, first of all, I do not want to make my trust of others contingent on their meeting my expectations of them. I do not want trust to become a bargain or exchange, like two parties entering into a contract: "You place your trust in me, and so I will place my trust in you. As long as you behave this way, I will continue to trust you." Instead, my trust is a gift that I wish to offer freely.

I do understand that generally trust should go both ways. But the way I look at it is that I am basing my trust in others in my own feelings of affection for the other person, not in their behavior. I care for someone, and there is a feeling of affection, therefore I choose to trust them.

Of course, this is not an easy understanding of trust to adopt. It entails a redefinition of what trust means. This redefinition can take place when we focus on the love and aspirations we have for the other person, rather than on how they do or do not behave toward us. We shift our attention from what we get to what we give.

It is true that sometimes other people behave in ways that hurt us. But even if we feel upset, our trust can remain steady, if it is anchored in love and if it was given without conditions. In chapter 3, "Healthy Relationships," I spoke of learning to love without any particular reason. When our love for another person is not contingent on anything they give or do, they can never give us a reason to stop loving them. When we trust in another person's fundamental goodness and their worth as a human being, then that trust will be deeply rooted enough to weather any storm.

By contrast, if trust is made dependent on fluctuating conditions, it is very difficult to sustain. One small disappointment, and the foundation of trust is shaken. So I think we need to be careful not to heap too many expectations and demands on the other person. Even if we are no longer on speaking terms with someone, we need to see that this other person, whom we trusted out of love, must still live. They still want to be happy. Just because they have disappointed us does not mean that we would want them to suffer. Even if trust is breached, we can keep our focus on our wish for their happiness, rather than on what we expected to get from them. This gives our long-term relationships a firm enough foundation to weather conflicts.

Our trust can be like the best aspiration we have for the other person. Our aspirations for their well-being can remain, regardless of what is going on between us and the other person at any given moment. In any case, relationships evolve a great deal over the course of a lifetime, and there will always be further transformations down the road. This is how I see it. For me, my trust is a permanent gift. Once I have offered it, it is given for good.

I think that a shift from valuing what we get, to valuing what we give, can serve us well in many aspects of our relationships. It can certainly help when we come into conflict with others, or when we are trying to help resolve others' conflicts. We might find it difficult to do this completely, but even small steps toward increasing the priority we give to others' well-being can move us away from conflict. Sincerely caring for the happiness of those on whom we depend for our own happiness might be one of the most powerful tools we can bring to our work to resolve conflicts. In a world of interdependence, it is surely also one of the wisest tools we can apply.

10 • Spiritual Paths
Integrating Life and Spirituality

I N THIS BOOK, I have been outlining what could be called a
kind of humanist spirituality. Of course, I am drawing on what
I have learned from Buddhist teachings. Yet everything I have
been saying is a logical consequence of the interdependence that
binds us to others and to the planet. You could come to these con-
clusions yourself, because they are grounded in observations and
experiences that anyone could have, regardless of religious orientation. When a truth is universal, it cannot belong to any single
religion—or any single secular view, either.

I am suggesting ways to look at the world and to live life that
do not require any particular religious affiliation. I am doing so
with the hope that this book might serve anyone who wishes to
live a fuller, more compassionate, and more meaningful life. Yet
there are also people who do yearn to make a deeper commitment
to a particular spiritual path. This chapter is for them.

In my own case, I was born in a Buddhist family. We were a
very spiritual family. I say "spiritual" rather than "religious," because we were highly respectful of something beyond the material
world that we perceived directly, and yet we knew very little of
religious ideologies or tenets. We were not entirely ignorant, but
the views we held and the principles we followed were very few
and very simple. This is the way I was raised as a boy.

Then, one day when I was around seven years old, a group

from my monastery arrived in our valley and told my family that I was the Karmapa. That event pretty much determined that I would be a Buddhist. What could I do? For me, there was no question of choosing which religion to adopt. I was simply stamped as a Buddhist. If you were suddenly told that you were the Karmapa, you too would have to accept that you were going to be Buddhist!

Although I did not undergo a process of exploring alternatives and selecting a spiritual path to follow, you do have this opportunity, if you wish to take it. In earlier times, it was taken for granted that people would adopt whatever religion their parents observed. This is still the case in more traditional cultures. But in much of the modern world, religious identity is a matter of individual choice, often made after a deliberate process of exploring different options. Selecting a religion or spiritual path is a major life decision. Some of you may end up rejecting religion and spirituality altogether. Others may remain with the religion you were born into, but with renewed confidence in its value for you personally. Yet others among you may find that a different spiritual path better suits your heart and your mind.

Today, quite a few people who were not born in Buddhist cultures or families are taking an interest in Buddhist teachings. I take this as a sign of the spirit of our age, with its acute awareness that there are many ways to explain the meaning of life and our place in the world.

Science and Religion

History tells us that human beings have been practicing religion for thousands of years, perhaps from the very beginning of human society. Evidently, cultivating a life of the spirit serves a fundamental human need; otherwise, religious traditions would not have formed part of human cultures throughout history. Nowadays, however, even as many people continue to find meaning in a religious or spiritual life, many others believe that religion is no longer relevant. It is a relic that belongs in the past, they say.

Some people think science should take the place of religion in the modern world, but many others, even great scientists, disagree. Albert Einstein once said, "Science without religion is lame, religion without science is blind." We need science. But we need religion, too. Scientific advancement brings consequences. Because of science, we have terrible nuclear weapons to deal with. Further, material progress has increased the disparity between rich and poor, to a point that seems almost unbridgeable. Without conscious thought and heartfelt direction, technology and science can potentially cause as much harm as good, and possibly more.

I think that science can be seen as our limbs—our hands and feet—while spirituality can serve as our eyes. Our hands and feet alone cannot tell us which direction to go. In fact, it can be dangerous to be efficient at moving ahead rapidly if we cannot see what lies ahead. We need to be able to foresee the consequences of scientific developments. We cannot think of science just as progress. We need to ask: Progress toward what?

Outer Knowledge, Inner Wisdom

Progress in technology and scientific research has been limited largely to the realm of external matter. The knowledge our generation has gained from all this research and study remains on an outer level—as if everything we need to know about life existed externally. As a result, we have developed a strong outward-looking orientation. In the process of making all these discoveries, we have failed to turn inward in order to develop wisdom and self-awareness. We do not ask: Who is making the discovery? Who is gaining the knowledge, and for what purpose? What kind of world do we wish to create, and what meaningful place do we envision for ourselves in that world? These are questions that religions aim to answer.

This is not to say that we should stop inquiring into the workings of the world around us. We just need to turn that same inquisitive gaze to the inner world. If we do so, we can come to truly know ourselves, and bring heart and mind together. To become more familiar with the nature of our own mind takes effort and commitment. When left to our own devices, we tend to remain very distracted. Our mind is so full of mental clutter that we fail to get a clear line of sight on the nature of our own mind. We have to make the space to look at ourselves. At times, we may also need to create distance from the busyness of our life and the array of goods that we tend to use to fill up that life. Given our habitual external orientation, sitting quietly with ourselves may take some getting used to.

Of course, it is also very important to truly see other human beings. But in order to see others well, it is sometimes necessary to see and know yourself first. Each religious tradition in the world offers some idea of the possible meanings of life and some methods for coming to know yourself better. Exploring different paths and adopting one as your religious philosophy or tradition is just a beginning. A religious philosophy or tradition only gives you a sort of introduction to the important issues. For example, the philosophy, epistemology, and metaphysics of the Buddhist traditions are vast and rich. The study of a philosophy or religion can be fascinating. But finding it interesting is not enough. You need to actively seek and find its truths for yourself.

There is a story about a supercomputer that was asked to calculate the meaning of life. The computer took many years to process this complex question, but at last it came up with an answer. It determined that the meaning of life is . . . the number 42. This was meant to be humorous, and of course, it really is laughable. No one else can settle the ultimate questions in life for us—least of all a machine.

We ourselves must engage personally in the process of discovering the meaning of our own life. It cannot be handed to us—either by a machine or by another person. Without our direct personal engagement, religion alone cannot solve the big questions in life for us. This is why personal experiences have such an important place in our spiritual path. I believe a spiritual path is most effective for us when we bring all our experiences along with us on that path.

To an outside observer, I might appear extremely religious. Because I spent my childhood first in a traditional society and then in a monastery receiving intensive religious training, some people may feel my religious beliefs must have been imposed on me. But that is not at all how I experienced it. I underwent a good deal of training in various aspects of Buddhist philosophy, but my feeling for religion came only later, and grew from my own experiences. This worked out fine in my case, but for most people I do not think being told how things are before gaining any experience for themselves is most effective. Rather, I think we should ground our religious understanding in our own experiences.

How can we do that? When we are exploring a particular religion or spiritual path, we can ask what it teaches us about who we are. Our spiritual path should help us to think profoundly about our life, and it should help us learn how to be happy. We can ask how those teachings help us understand the experiences we have had in life so far. Even after we have selected a particular path, we can continue to bring whatever arises in our life to our religious teachings. When spirituality is anchored deeply in our experience of life in this way, it can become a central moving force in our life.

Authentic Discovery

If I were asked the question, "What religion are you?" it would seem very odd if I did not say, "I'm a Buddhist." After all, people look to me as a Buddhist leader! To keep things simple, it is easier for me to say, "I am a Buddhist." Yet that is not how I see myself. Rather, I see myself as a follower of the Buddha. I aspire to follow in the Buddha's footsteps. To hold on to the label of "Buddhist" and wave it like a banner is something else altogether.

When I say I wish to follow in the Buddha's footsteps, the key point for me is that the Buddha used his own intelligence to discover the meaning of life within himself. He did not discover it from texts written by someone else, or from any formalized set of rules. He found it within himself, within his own noble heart. We all have the potential to do this.

The discovery of who you are cannot just be extracted from texts or rituals. Even if you are contemplating words you have read or heard others say, you have to discover the truth of their meaning for yourself. You must discover each piece of it for yourself—and you have to put the pieces together yourself, too, because you will not find what you seek by just taking up something that has already been assembled for you.

There is great transformative power in the act of discovery. No founder of any religion was a follower. The Buddha became the Buddha because he discovered important truths for himself. Many remarkable people following within his tradition also came to that understanding themselves. The same is true of the founders and remarkable followers of every other major world religion. Each brought forth new insights and understanding. Everyone is capable of that; you just need the right conditions. Joining a religion or studying its wisdom can be one of those conditions. But I have studied Buddhist philosophy for over a decade, and I can tell you that such study is not sufficient in order to find true meaning. Only if your own understanding is rooted profoundly within will you be able to awaken spiritually. Only you can understand your life and find its deepest meaning.

The historical moment always shapes and informs the way spiritual teachings are presented. Following something taught in the past to people in different social and historical circumstances can never be the same as living spiritually here and now. The simple fact is, in the realm of spiritual matters, you have to arrive at your own understanding yourself. That is, you must personally and actively engage in your spiritual path, whatever that path may be. There really is no other way.

I want to be clear that seeking your own understanding does not mean rejecting all established spiritual paths. Many people feel that organized religions are problematic—or even hopelessly flawed. They might even think that they could assemble a better religion for themselves by picking and choosing bits they like from different religions. I do not think this is realistic. It simply does not work as we think it might. Instead of something holistic that transforms us, it just yields a patchwork that pleases us. This can become a kind of spiritual consumerism.

Worse, it can be dangerous. Bits that you thought would be beneficial for you can turn out to be ineffective or even harmful if you apply them out of context. When you extract practices from a gradual path of transformation, they might not have the same effect outside of their intended sequence. Our spiritual path has to unfold organically—and we have to be receptive to going where it leads us, step-by-step.

Spiritual Teacher as Friend

The process of clearing away the obstacles to self-knowledge is not haphazard. If we do not have the necessary conditions, spiritual awakening will not simply happen randomly. We already have the main condition—our noble heart. But we need to actively bring together the rest of the causes and conditions. Spiritual teachings are one crucial condition. They can come from a spiritual teacher, from elders or from books. The natural world in its play of elements can offer us teachings. Even the sound of running water in a stream can teach us. It can evoke the truth of constant change. The smoothness of the stones in the riverbed can inspire us with a teaching that consistent, gradual effort can reshape even the hardest structures.

When looking for a spiritual teacher, in my view the starting point should be that they are a good person. You should consider not just whether the teacher is an educated and knowledgeable person, but also whether he or she is a genuinely good-hearted person who has real affection for you. This is hard to tell from the outside; a teacher doesn't come wearing a sign saying, "I am good-hearted."

People have different personalities. Rather than looking for teachers with a particular personality, you should examine whether or not they are kind, and whether or not they have a positive impact on others. Teachers can be reclusive or reserved, so you'll have to use your own judgment to determine whether they care for you or inspire you in a positive way.

How long should you examine a potential teacher? This is not easy to say. It is not as if they immediately take care of all your spiritual or emotional needs. The connection has to be developed over time.

My own personal feeling is that there are actually two considerations in selecting a spiritual teacher. One is this initial process of examination. The other is trust. The relationship between teacher and student is a relationship that you have to cultivate. It is not something that you discover already fully developed. You let the teacher get to know you, including your faults. At the same time, you gain confidence that the teacher will continue to care for you as a student. It is important that you feel able to trust your teacher, and you yourself must also be trustworthy. In a relationship between spiritual teacher and student, trust has to be mutual.

The Place of Community

Community can also play an important role in your spiritual life. This does not mean you need to set off on a quest to find a spiritual community to join. Instead, you might approach it with the simple thought that it would be good to have a friend. It would be even better to have a friend who shares your spiritual interests. Having a few such friends would be better still.

I could put it another way: We need good friends in life, people who encourage and inspire us, and whom we encourage and inspire. We need trustworthy friends. It is difficult to create trust in this world. And yet as I described in chapter 9, "Conflict Resolution," trust is extremely important for the sustenance of our being. I myself have had a difficult course in life, leaving everything behind and facing many obstacles. Yet I still have trust. I feel that trusting others is essential for my sustenance.

We are social beings. Each individual is dependent on others. It is important to have close friends who give us moral support and who bring out the good qualities we have within us. This is much more important than sharing a label or joining an organization. This is also true both in friendships and in the teacher-student relationship. A spiritual teacher has to be a good friend to you.

Keep It Simple

Once you have committed to a particular path, I suggest that you look for the simplest way forward. You should make things accessible and approachable in your religious community and in your personal practice, rather than more complicated.

Keep it simple. The life of the spirit is actually very basic and easy. We often don't appreciate that. In the beginning, our spiritual path may strike us as very simple and perfectly clear. But then, after we have been practicing it for a few years, we sometimes find ourselves going backward, and moving away from that initial simplicity. The spiritual breakthroughs we experience may simply consist in rediscovering what we had seen in the beginning.

Spiritual discovery is not a matter of finding wisdom out there somewhere. It is a matter of discovering what already exists within us. Like cleaning the surface of a stone inscription, the more you clean it, the more the original carving becomes apparent. We are like that stone. With spiritual practice, instead of gaining something we did not have before, we gradually make ourselves clearer to ourselves.

Go Ahead and Doubt

Especially for those who are newly adopting a spiritual path, there is a tendency to take that path too seriously. There is a real danger of becoming self-righteous about it, and then clinging to it. I suggest taking it easy. Leave yourself the freedom to discover. Find a balance between plunging in completely, and staying disengaged.

To ensure we maintain a wide perspective, we should guard against becoming dogmatic. I think it is very good to doubt. When you have doubts, you question and seek answers. You want to hear what others have to say. Do make sure to ask questions, and study to clarify anything that is unclear to you. This requires you to stay open-minded. Go ahead and doubt!

Buddhist texts speak of two kinds of doubt, one that is useful for spiritual growth, the other not. The one that is not very useful is a dismissive sort of doubt; the other is a more inquisitive doubt. With the dismissive sort, you have basically decided for yourself that something is wrong and false, but you still let others present their case. You only halfheartedly listen to what they have to say, because you are already inclined to dismiss it. With the more impartial or inquisitive sort of doubt, you have the feeling that what they say just might be true, but you want to make sure. With this second kind of doubt, you are receptive, but there is a part of your mind that listens very carefully, wanting to ascertain the truth for yourself.

We need to get things clear so that we know how to relate them to our own experiences. When we let ourselves question and take a lively interest, we will remain actively engaged in our own process of spiritual awakening. On that basis, we will be able to remain fully attentive to opportunities for growth. We will begin to connect our whole life to spiritual growth.

Staying Mindful of Happiness

The primary aim of a spiritual path is true happiness. Everything else is secondary. We could ask ourselves how we can create authentic, real happiness. Simply because we have a noble heart and human intelligence, we have excellent opportunities to find genuine happiness in life. But happiness, like spiritual awakening, is not created haphazardly. We do not gain lasting happiness by merely following the dictates of our fluctuating emotions. And we do not find it by mindlessly repeating our habitual patterns. We need to apply our innate intelligence and wisdom in order to discover the meaning of our life. Yet we cannot discover it solely through intellectual analysis, for happiness is not created by intellect alone. We must engage our heart.

We can make every step we take in life—every single experience—an opportunity to grow spiritually. If we stay present, even the bending of blades of grass as the wind passes can awaken us to the truth of interdependence. When you take the time to be present with yourself, you can experience many such moments of quiet discovery. This requires you to stop chasing after things, people, and experiences, and to cultivate a capacity to be at rest.

This habit of chasing is strong. Life in the twenty-first century seems to encourage that. We find little or no time for reflection or prayer, because we are so caught up in pursuing all our different goals and juggling their competing demands. When a session of meditation or quiet reflection is squeezed into our busy calendars, it is hard to settle our mind. Treating our spiritual life like another item on our list of activities to accomplish is not an effective approach. The spiritual practice will feel rushed, and can become a matter of obligation—something we need to finish so we can move through the rest of the items on our to-do list.

While we need to be careful not to treat our spiritual practice like another of our daily chores, we should also take care not to set it off from the rest of our life. If our life is to be transformed by our practice, there should not be such a gap between our spiritual practice and our day-to-day experiences. Rather, spirituality should be merged with the rest of our life.

Spirituality is a process of self-discovery. You cannot discover what is not within your own experience. Your spirituality has to be developed within you. When you see religion or spirituality as distinct from your life itself, then at most your life can be shaped by religion. But instead, your life should shape your religion. You understand your religion—maybe even the whole universe—through your own life.

Sometimes there is an expectation that spiritual practice consists of some techniques that we deploy to make our life spiritual. If we can remain attentive to what matters most, to our spiritual priorities, then spiritual and "nonspiritual" activities should not feel separate.

One of our most important challenges in life is to remain mindful of who we are and what we are doing. To keep this awareness present all the time is a great support for spiritual growth. One aspect of a spiritual life is to live consciously. For that, we need to be as fully aware as possible. Without mindfulness, we end up sleepwalking through life. We act without realizing what we are doing.

The danger of knowing many spiritual techniques but lacking mindfulness can be imagined with the analogy of a great swimmer who suddenly falls in the water. It might happen so suddenly that he forgets where he is and who he is. He might even forget in his panic that he is a great swimmer. He could forget that he belongs on the dry land, and that he should swim to reach it. There is no mindfulness, and all his techniques are rendered useless at precisely the moment they are most needed.

Who Do You Want to Be?

I would like to give you an example of what I mean by bringing our experiences to our spiritual path. Maintaining your equanimity throughout the day can be one way to do so. I spoke earlier of my elderly attendant. He is in his seventies and I am in my twenties. His intentions are very good, but we are of entirely different generations, and different things seem important to each of us. We live together, and to me, it seems that he nags me over every little thing. I only wear monastic robes, every day. But he still picks out clothes for me to wear, saying, "Don't wear those robes. Wear these." It is like this all day, every day. It could easily become annoying, but I have learned not to take it too seriously. Really, it is funny. I have the option of feeling annoyed or laughing at the situation.

When you are cultivating equanimity as part of your spiritual practice, it helps to remember that you are under no obligation to take everything so seriously. Being tense and deadly serious about working with anger makes it even harder. Instead, you can bring in a quality of lightness. Being playful about the situations you are in is very helpful. You can make even anger into a game. But in order for this game to work, you do need to commit to playing this game fully, with your body, speech, and mind. What is the use in sitting there and saying, "I don't want to get angry," with teeth clenched and your face clouded over with anger? You may have some good reasons to be angry, but you don't have to hold on to them so tightly. At any moment, you can just drop them. Recognizing that you have the option to let go, and then deciding to do so, can be considered a spiritual practice.

To maintain your equanimity when you feel yourself getting annoyed, you can imagine that there are two people inside of you. One wants to get angry, and the other doesn't. Many things can help you see this, even a comic-book hero like Spider-Man. Imagine you are Peter Parker, and you have two Spider-Man costumes that you could put on at any moment. Your tranquil self is like the red Spider-Man costume. (Red Spider-Man is the good guy, remember.) Your anger is like the black Spider-Man costume; you become the bad guy when you put it on. Which one do you want to put on? Which one do you want to wear with your body, speech, and mind? You always have both options, and can choose which one to take out of your closet.

This is a very simple approach really, but it will require some effort. Consciously remind yourself of the choices you want to make, so that you can react wisely when the time comes. Staying aware in the different situations you face and responding to them wisely—that is one way to merge your experiences with your spiritual path.

Breaking Down Barriers

As you pursue your own particular spiritual path, you do so in a world of great religious diversity. It is important to ensure that your religious commitment does not prevent you from feeling closely connected to others who do not share your particular path. Even though we all share a single world, when we hold tightly to religious labels, these labels can keep us worlds apart. For all that religions can potentially offer us, they can also become a major cause of animosity and social strife, rather than a way to end them.

We are all united by the simple fact that we are human beings. Religious teachings seek to address us on a universal human level. Yet clinging to a specific religious identity might move you further from the spirit of that religion's teachings. When religions end up dividing us, it is a sure sign that something has gone terribly wrong. To guard against that, keeping a wide focus on our shared humanity is extremely important.

For instance, we have come to the point where people equate Islam with terrorism. People become afraid of ordinary human beings just because they are Muslims. Every winter I go to Bodh

Gaya, India—the most sacred site for Buddhists—to hold the Kagyu Monlam, our gathering for world peace. A mosque was recently built adjacent to the Bodhi tree, where the Buddha attained enlightenment and where we hold our prayers. Sometimes during our breaks for tea, we can hear the Muslim call to prayer being broadcast over a loudspeaker system. At first, some people felt uncomfortable and threatened by this. But that is strange: we are there to pray, and they are also being called to prayer. We inevitably pass Muslims on the street when we go to and from our prayers, and the quickest glance is enough to affirm that they are human beings just like us. But if our labels blind us to that obvious fact, a lot of wild ideas can develop, and the divisions between "us" and "them" can begin to seem very solid. For this reason, we have to be very careful about how we wield such labels.

In 2001, the huge Bamiyan Buddha statues in Afghanistan were intentionally demolished. From a certain perspective within Islam, these statues were offensive instruments of idol worship, while to Buddhists they were reminders of sacred principles and the very best of our innate human potential. Basically, we Buddhists use physical images in our spiritual practice, while Muslims worship without images. Clinging to either position was creating a wall between people. But they are just statues. Allowing ourselves to be pitted against each other over a statue—now that is really clinging to biases.

Personally, I do not see a basis for treating religious differences this way. A while after the Bamiyan Buddhas were destroyed, I had the opportunity to meet with an Afghan youth group working for peace. I suggested to them that we might view the coming down of the Bamiyan Buddhas as bringing down the walls between all peoples. If the presence of those statues was setting us at odds, perhaps we could see it as useful that they were brought down. This is how I felt about it.

Walls come up between people when we attach more importance to the form of our religious identities than to the substance of what they teach us. When spiritual beliefs are used to build up walls between people, this is a total misunderstanding of the purpose of spirituality. Spirituality should mean coming closer to yourself. When this happens, you become closer to others, too. Spirituality and religion should dismantle discrimination and labels, not shore them up. It should break, not create, barriers between people.

Embracing Diversity

Living in a society with a diversity of religious beliefs is a fine opportunity to put our own tolerance, respect, and love into practice. Tolerance, respect, and love are values shared by all the major world religions. Surely most people who are strictly secular also hold to the view that respect for others is an important ethical value.

We can use a simple analogy to think about religious difference. The fact that we like a certain food does not mean everyone else has to like it. We do not get upset with our friends if they do not share our taste in food. When we eat in a restaurant together, we do not insist that they order the same dishes as we do, do we? We want them to eat food that suits them, and that they will enjoy.

We are human beings. We are neighbors. We all share the same planet, and breathe the same atmosphere. We are warmed by the same sun, and enjoy the soft light of the same moon. Because of this, we will always have things in common. Spirituality ought to heighten our awareness of all that we hold in common. It should enhance our recognition of the basic worth of all human beings.

We will also always have things that distinguish us. The main consideration should be whether another person's religion is contributing to their well-being, not whether or not we agree with its tenets. The differences between religious beliefs are relatively superficial. Although the lineages and texts differ, in essence Christianity, Buddhism, Judaism, Hinduism, Islam, and the other world religions share many similarities. This is easy to see when we consider their ethical values and their emphasis on the awakening of human beings' highest potential.

Whether or not we think the tenets of other religions are true is not the point. The point is that if we care about others' happiness, we can be pleased that their religion is serving to bring them some happiness. If their religion or spiritual path is contributing to their well-being, that is what really matters.

I keep copies of the scriptures of each of the major religions of the world in my room. I have a personal practice of my own that I do with them. I take each scripture from the shelf and hold it in my hands as I make the aspiration: "Many millions of people have placed their faith and hope in the teachings contained in this scripture. May these teachings become a true vehicle for those who make their own aspirations through them. May these teachings be a vehicle that brings them all happiness."

11 • Sustainable Compassion
Grounding Ourselves in Courage and Joy

T HE HEART OF EVERY PERSON on this planet yearns at all times to be free of suffering. We all have this wish, in every moment of our existence. Our longing to be happy and free of suffering is among the most basic things we share.

The entire purpose of the spiritual training in the Buddhist tradition practiced in Tibet is to be able to free all beings from their suffering. We call a person who is working toward this goal a "bodhisattva." This Sanskrit term describes someone who has developed his or her compassion to the point where it is spontaneous and unconditional toward all beings. Bodhisattvas are true examples of open-heartedness. When we observe them, we see what we will be like when our noble heart is fully open. Bodhisattvas feel a deep aspiration to bring happiness to all beings everywhere. They find their own happiness in standing at the side of anyone who suffers, to offer them relief and to help them find a way out of their suffering. As long as they see that they can benefit others, bodhisattvas are content—in fact, delighted—to stay put in the hardest of situations in order to work for the well-being of others. We too can aspire to bring this same vast courage and noble-heartedness into our relationships and all our activity. The only real difference between us and bodhisattvas is that they are already basing their lives fully in their noble heart.

Long ago in Tibet, there was very little exposure to the outside world. A few people had heard the word "America," but "America" could have been a town or a whole continent for all we knew. There was really no idea of its size or what the strange-sounding word actually referred to. The name "Russia" was better known. Our idea about "Russia" was that in evil times to come, the Russians would appear and eat us alive! It sounds like a fairy tale told to children, but that is what people in Tibet used to say about Russians.

Yet despite this narrow view of the world outside Tibet, people were bighearted. Their hearts could be as wide open as the sky. Tibetans imagined that wherever there was blue sky, there were sentient beings. And wherever there were sentient beings, they knew there would be suffering and a yearning for happiness. So they felt they should make aspirations for all sentient beings—who are so numerous that they fill all space—to find happiness and be free of suffering. Without any real contact or clear idea of who, what, or where those others were, Tibetans could extend their hearts so they were wide enough to encompass all space, and could aspire to be able to end the suffering of all beings and bring them happiness. This is the dichotomy: people can have limited knowledge, but infinitely expansive hearts.

In my own case, I am obviously not in a position to benefit all beings of the world. Even though I know this, I still nurture the aspiration to be able to do so. It would be truly wonderful if I could actually benefit others. But even if I cannot, love and compassion are still urgently needed in this world. If I live my life cultivating compassion and love, I think that this might be a source of hope and courage for some people. Just being alive in the world and holding love in my heart can be an expression of my caring for others. Even that can be significant. I nourish this small thought. Or maybe it's not small, but it is simple—very simple on the one hand, but on the other hand, vast and expansive.

Our Noble Heart of Compassion

Earlier I described the possibility of seeing your life as something that extends far beyond yourself, connecting you to many others. If you can cultivate the outlook that you are a part of others, your suffering can decrease and your courage increase. The painful egocentrism that complicates all your relationships can be greatly eased. It can bring an element of true closeness and intense love to all your encounters with others. In this way, when you see yourself as not just connected to but actually part of all beings, this alone can transform your experience of the world and your relationship with every single being in it. You can live in a state of perfect harmony with the world. This is the ultimate form of emotional stability and lasting happiness.

We make the aspiration in Tibetan:

When I am happy, I offer that happiness to others.
May that joy and delight fill all the world.
When there is suffering, may I carry it all.

Developing such boundless compassion might sound like a huge challenge. But compassion is not something new that we need to acquire or engineer for ourselves. It is already present within each one of us. No matter how seemingly bad a person is, they still have compassion as a fundamental, integral part of their nature. We all do. For that reason, our compassion will never be depleted. It has a sustaining power in and of itself.

Although we all have compassion as part of our nature, there are differences in how we develop and apply it. People have different aptitudes and aspirations that shape how their compassion manifests. Initially our compassionate action will take place within those limitations. Yet there are many contemplative practices we can use to extend our compassion. In this regard, there is a particular role for aspirations or prayers in which we generate the wish to be able to move beyond our present limitations, and do more in the future to bring about the happiness of others. It is my own heartfelt aspiration that all of your sincere aspirations be fulfilled in the future, and I offer you all my support to that end.

What "All Beings" Really Means

When our compassion has grown past our personal limitations, it can become a limitless wish to benefit all beings—each and every being, everywhere. This does not just mean the people we like and feel close to. It does not even mean benefiting just the seven billion human beings in our world. In Buddhist terms, "all beings" implies all the humans and animals on our planet, but also all beings possessed of sentience in our galaxy, in our entire universe, and ultimately perhaps in other universes. We extend our compassion anywhere that there are sentient beings.

Such vast compassion entails a sense of responsibility for bringing about the happiness of all beings—any sentient being, anywhere, any time. We have been talking about reversing the destruction done to our planet, ending world hunger, or bringing about justice in our food systems and social systems, as ways to care for all beings. Although we can already begin moving in that direction today, these are not goals that we can accomplish in a single day, or a week, or even perhaps within our entire lifetime. Making our long-term vision of a better world a reality entails some exceedingly long-term goals. Therefore the compassion that moves us to work toward these goals needs to be sustained for an exceedingly long time. This makes it particularly important for us to ensure that our compassion is sustainable.

I recognize that this wish to create a better society, end all the suffering of all beings everywhere, and protect the entire planet may not seem particularly feasible. But whether or not we accomplish such goals in our lifetime, it is nevertheless deeply meaningful to cultivate such a vast sense of responsibility, and the wholehearted wish to be able to benefit others. This outlook is so wholesome and noble that it is worth developing, regardless of the probability of actually accomplishing such a vast vision.

Recognizing the nobility of this outlook, we can cultivate a compassion that is both intense and stable enough to carry us forward, despite the magnitude of the task ahead. We can start by reinforcing our conviction that any being with sentience by definition experiences feelings of pleasure and pain. Simply because they feel pain and yearn to be free of it and have the capacity to feel happiness, we should respect their experiences and value them. We really need look for no other reason.

Once we begin to truly value others' happiness, if an opportunity arises for us to give others happiness or protect them from suffering, we will be ready to do so. If we are able to nurture a sense of continual readiness to act, we will not miss opportunities to benefit others. Even if we cannot immediately ensure the welfare of all beings, any time we see an opportunity to benefit any particular being, we will be eagerly waiting to act on our compassion. When we notice someone hungry in the street, we will look at once for something to offer them. We will become proactive and start carrying healthy foods to give them, or seek out a local food kitchen to support. As long as we aspire to benefit others, we will continually find opportunities to do so, and happily seize them whenever they present themselves. Thus this aspiration in itself has great significance and actual power.

Coloring Life with Compassion

Compassion that is sustainable must last beyond momentary bursts of inspiration. It must be enduring, so we have to learn ways to keep our compassion going beyond the point where it begins to wane. There is no single technique that will serve in all circumstances. Once we are committed to carrying true compassion into our life, we can embrace it in even the smallest acts. We can color our whole life with kindness, transforming our everyday activities and suffusing our everyday ways of being with human warmth. This can happen. Our life can be translated into love.

Anything can be an opportunity to do this. If we hear a bird singing, that sound can remind us of compassion, awakening a wish to offer that bird our love. We can use our eyes as well as our ears. Whatever we see can be a basis for us to let the language of loving-kindness flow through our life. In fact, we can use all the five senses as avenues opening onto a warmhearted outlook.

We Tibetans have a saying: "You can enact compassion with every step you take." It is not sufficient for your compassion to remain within you, as an attitude or an inner practice. You must express it through your speech and through your physical actions. Every single step can become a manifestation of your compassion.

Beyond your own body and speech, whatever you create can also be a means of expressing love: your poetry, music, or artwork. Whatever you do on a daily basis—cooking, eating, sleeping, getting dressed—all of these can be infused with love and compassion. Just going for a walk can be permeated with an open-hearted outlook. When all that you do stems from the motivating forces of love and compassion, then your actions become truly sustainable.

Some people think compassion is too difficult to sustain in actual practice. It may seem so when we focus on being effective in our care for others. For example, imagine that a stray dog has been hit by a car and wounded. Its wounds become infested with maggots. If I help the dog by getting rid of the maggots, this hurts the maggots. If I don't, the maggots harm the dog. What to do? This is a question that I've been asked more than once, and there is no easy answer. We seem to be caught in a vicious circle, and lack the wisdom to find a way forward. Such tough choices do make compassion seem tricky to apply and to sustain. We need to be spacious in how we think through such dilemmas. However, we also need to recognize that these cases are exceptions. For the most part, compassion is not all that complicated to apply.

Living compassionately only becomes tricky when we expect that our efforts will meet with success every time. When we feel compassion, we naturally want to do something to remove the suffering we perceive. But that wish cannot always translate directly into results. Apart from our lack of wisdom as to how to enact our compassion in certain situations, we might also lack the material resources needed to solve a given problem. Even if we do have something to give, there can be other obstacles.

Setting aside the complex task of bringing about social changes, even something as simple as giving out candies with a joyful wish to share their sweetness with strangers can be difficult to do. Your offer might well be met with a suspicious frown. But the kindness of your gesture remains, even if the gift is not accepted. The sheer goodness of your aspiration outweighs any outer obstacles, no matter how big or small. The point is to love and to feel compassion, and to make those wholesome feelings the basis for joyful action. This allows you to sustain compassion within yourself, regardless of whether or not your efforts to benefit others meet with success in outer terms.

Caring for Others, Caring for Self

As I mentioned earlier, when it comes to acting on our compassion, everyone has his or her own individual inclinations and abilities. Some people may be particularly moved by the plight of the homeless; others may feel more inspired to work for animal rights. Our inclinations will guide our actions, and our abilities will also place limits on what we are able to do at any given point in our development of compassion.

Even when we are acting in ways that primarily serve our own interests, there are better and worse ways to do so. While striving to accomplish our own goals, we can also seek to bring about others' well-being at the same time. If we are unable to benefit others, at the very least we should make sure that we do not harm them as we go about securing our own interests. In any case, whether we are seeking to benefit others or just ourselves, we can only do so within the limits of our personal abilities. I think this is important to bear in mind, so that we do not become disappointed with ourselves or frustrated by the lack of material results.

There is another way to think of the relationship between working for ourselves and working for others. These two orientations do not need to be in conflict with one another. We can speak of compassion as facing in two directions: outward or inward. If the face of compassion is turned inward, toward oneself, the attitude would be what in Buddhism is called renunciation, which is defined as the wish to turn away from everything that causes suffering. When we renounce, in Buddhist terms, we are not rejecting things themselves; we are rejecting our attachment to those things. We are renouncing whatever causes us pain and dissatisfaction, and this includes the endless pursuit of empty sense pleasures. Renunciation is a wise way of caring for ourselves. If compassion is turned outward, this is what we more commonly call compassion. We want others to be free of suffering as well as everything that causes their suffering.

Compassion in this sense is like a coin with two faces. The coin is made of the same material throughout; it just faces two different directions. In both cases, there is a simple wish to bring suffering to an end, either your own suffering or that of others. The caring attitude is essentially identical.

There is a simple way to gauge whether or not what you are feeling is authentic compassion. If the concern you feel for others is genuine compassion, then it can also be applied to yourself with no change in quality or intensity. If the compassion you feel for yourself is genuine, then it can also be applied to others without changing. Your compassionate wish to see an end to suffering would be the same whether the suffering was yours or another's. But if your "compassion" comes mixed with a subtle sense of superiority toward the person you see suffering, then the feeling would change when you directed it at yourself instead of others. You would obviously no longer be able to feel superior to yourself. If your experience changes when you direct your gaze inward rather than outward, this is a sign that what you feel is not real compassion. Rather, it might be an effort to boost your own ego or avoid your own problems by focusing on others who you believe have greater problems than you do. This is not what we would call compassion. It might instead be a form of condescension, or even codependency.

We need to be able to place ourselves and others on even ground, so that the intensity and quality of our care for others becomes similar to our care for ourselves. For example, if we look at others and find them worthy of our love and care, but then look at ourselves and dislike what we see, this is unhealthy. By the same token, if we find ourselves to be wonderful and worth caring for, but dislike what we see in others, this is also unhealthy. When we can see ourselves and others both as fully worthy of care, then we can call this compassion.

Concern for Victims and Abusers Alike

Ultimately, for compassion to be complete and unconditional, we also have to be able to feel it for those who harm others in significant ways. This can be very challenging. We tend to be generous in opening our heart to victims, yet quite closed off toward their abusers. I can offer some suggestions for working on this, but I do want to acknowledge that this is easier said than done.

One place we can start is by recognizing that those who harm others are lacking a certain kind of freedom. We should understand that it would be impossible for individuals who hurt or terrorize others to act in that way if they were not overpowered by severe emotional afflictions.

This is true even of the most notorious murderers—they kill while under the control of serious mental problems, strong emotional upheavals, or some other powerful negative influence. They have fallen under the sway of a painful state of fury. They are harming others while they themselves are in a state of complete deprivation of authentic freedom. We can even say that they have become the first victim of their own anger. Their anger is much stronger than they are, and it has taken them over.

I realize this may sound difficult, but when we understand the reality of their situation, we ought to feel a heightening of our compassion when we observe people acting in such terrible ways. After all, their actions are a result of their own lack of freedom to control their own minds.

Although it may be hard to see at the time, that is not their true nature. The last thing sane people want to do is to inflict suffering on themselves. However, once people have fallen into the tight grip of mental afflictions, they bring pain and disaster on themselves and others. We know that one of the most painful forms of suffering is the lack of freedom. Such people have no freedom; they are enslaved by hideous mental afflictions. They follow the dictates of their distorted, confused, addicted, habitual outlook. This is a very painful state to be in.

Distinguishing between Person and Emotion

All of us might feel annoyed and get upset from time to time, but we can still retain some sense of identity apart from that anger. By contrast, serial killers, child abusers, rapists, and other people who inflict pain on others are utterly unable to pull themselves away from their own rage, hatred, and other destructive emotions. They literally cannot distance themselves from their emotions at all. They suffer from a serious distortion of reality, and cannot distinguish between what they feel at that particular moment, and the actual reality of who they are and what is going on. They can't be viewed the way we ordinarily view people. We should never in any way condone their actions, but neither should we confuse those actions with the individuals themselves.

There was a man who lived during the time of the Buddha whose life illustrates this point. There was an immensely strong-willed person named Angulimala. The overwhelming force of his own mental afflictions led him astray. Somehow he conceived of the idea that he would attain great spiritual powers if he killed a thousand people. He became completely determined to keep killing until he had reached a thousand victims. He was convinced that this would be the height of spiritual accomplishment. He cut a thumb from each of his murder victims, and wore them strung around his neck as a garland, and thus became known by the name "Angulimala," which means "Garland of Fingers" in Sanskrit.

Angulimala persisted until he had killed 999 people, and was then looking for his final victim. By this time, of course, he was so notorious that people ran the moment they saw him. If he was known to have entered an area, people feared to walk outdoors and stayed locked inside. The only one who did not hide from him was his loving mother. She still felt great concern for him, and was worried that he would go hungry. Seeing that no one else would do so, she went to bring him some food, and as soon as he saw her approaching, Angulimala decided to kill her. This murder would complete his quest for a thousand victims, and he thought that killing his own mother would be a fittingly spectacular pinnacle to his achievement.

The Buddha observed Angulimala turning on his own mother, and intervened. He said, "Rather than kill your mother, you should come after me."

Angulimala thought that killing the Buddha would be an even more magnificent finale than killing his mother, so he immediately abandoned his pursuit of her and went after the Buddha. But Angulimala couldn't catch up with the Buddha. This serial killer called out, "Stop! Don't go so fast."

The Buddha replied: "I have stopped. You are the one still moving, driven forward by your mental afflictions."

At that very moment, Angulimala gained the clarity to see for the first time that he and his mental afflictions were separate. He and his murderous impulses were not the same thing. This realization struck Angulimala like a lightning bolt, and he was stopped in his tracks. The deluded emotions simply lost their grip on him. He went on to become a disciple of the Buddha, and eventually became one of the most remarkable Buddhist monks of the day.

In one sense, we are not so different from Angulimala. We too harbor the illusion that our emotional upheavals are an indivisible part of us. But they are not at all inseparable from us. As long as we recall this, it is always possible to cast these mental afflictions aside, even under such terrible circumstances as Angulimala's.

It may seem impossible to ever forgive someone who caused such terrible harm and made such hideous mistakes. But when we know that they did what they did because they were controlled by their afflictions, we have a basis for forgiving the person. It may not be easy, but it is possible. However, because we know that the harm was caused by the person's mental afflictions, we should never forgive the mental afflictions, and neither do we approve the person's actions. Of course, this is very challenging to put into practice, but it is very much worth trying, because the benefits of extending our compassion to all beings are so great—and the harm to ourselves of harboring resentment are so great, too.

When we find ourselves in circumstances where an individual or a group of people are seeking to harm us, we can respond by deepening our resolve not to engage in such behavior ourselves. In this way, we can actually turn such adverse situations to our own advantage spiritually and emotionally.

How can we do this? We can reflect on why we dislike the behavior of those who harm us. It is because it is wrong and negative. Because of the particular way they are behaving, we may feel we are justified in disliking them as a person. But we should reflect that we were not born disliking them. We developed this dislike based on specific actions or qualities that we saw them displaying. We can reflect that we would dislike those qualities or behavior in anyone—even ourselves.

We can then ask ourselves why we would ever wish to have that quality in our own mind, or act in that way toward others. We would have given ourselves grounds to dislike ourselves. Since we feel this is wrong in others, we would become wrong in our own eyes if we acted in a similar way. This is not a question of feeling we are better than others, but rather of not wanting to behave in ways that we dislike. Therefore when we see such qualities or mistaken conduct in others, we can redouble our efforts to ensure that we ourselves do not allow such qualities to take root in our own heart in the slightest way.

Enthusiasm for the Long Haul

Enthusiasm is a powerful support of our compassion. When we feel enthusiasm, we can easily persevere in our efforts to help others. The way to awaken our enthusiasm is to reflect on the benefits of working for others, rather than the results of our particular efforts. To draw our motivation from the results of our actions is a particularly grave mistake in the case of compassion, because the cultivation of compassion is not an area where we can expect to see instant results.

Our compassionate outlook has to be fashioned bit by bit, slowly and with great care. It cannot be instantly mass-produced. After all, compassion is a mental state, not a machine. Mental cultivation takes time; it takes patience and endurance. We need to commit to it for the long haul.

This can be an issue for us, as we seem to be living in an era of quick fixes. Our consumer culture is infatuated with the idea that results will materialize instantly, and will be material and tangible.

When it comes to spiritual development, I think this orientation is potentially very harmful. Many of the most profound results of our compassion will not be outwardly perceptible. After all, compassion is not like throwing a punch at the world and seeing the black eye at once! Gentle and caring action works very differently from that.

In order to maintain our enthusiasm, it is extremely helpful to be clear what the ongoing and incremental benefits of compassion are. If you are absolutely sure about the benefits of cultivating this deeply wholesome outlook, you will take joy in your efforts even when you do not see huge results from your compassionate action. If your actions are based on a clear awareness of the long-term impact of your compassion, even if you don't succeed in your benevolent plans, there is never any cause for regret or guilt. After all, you have certainly done nothing wrong. Even if your compassionate actions produce no visible results, you can take joy in the awareness of the nobility of your efforts. As you reflect on how greatly meaningful it is to cultivate compassion, and as you consider the profound benefits of doing so, you will gain increasing confidence and courage. You will be empowered with the knowledge that your compassionate actions have value in and of themselves.

When you view your life from this perspective, your compassion will be sustainable under any circumstances. After all, compassion is always right there, as part of your nature. As you allow compassion to fill your heart and come to the forefront of your life, everything you encounter can become a condition for compassion to increase. Compassion can permeate your smallest gestures. And whenever the opportunity arises to act to benefit others in larger ways, you will be fully ready to do so—because compassion prepares you with a sense of responsibility for others' happiness and an urgent wish to act to accomplish it.

Just nurture your compassion and hold it ready to translate into action whenever possible. Beyond that, it is best not to focus on results. In fact, you will enjoy great benefits even when there are no external results to show for your efforts. The attitude of compassion itself is so deeply wholesome and meaningful that it is worth cultivating and preserving, regardless of the outcome of your compassionate action.

Compassion itself is noble.

12 • Living the Teachings

THIS IS OUR LAST CHAPTER together, for now. After this, I will leave you to continue cultivating the habit of extending your love and compassion outward to all beings. As you increase your awareness of your own noble heart in your everyday activities, it will become a central force in your life. Every single contact you have with another being can call you back to your love and compassion. When you hear a dog barking or whining, you will be able to rouse a feeling of love for that animal, thinking, "This is the cry of a being who is dear to me." That thought can remind you of the suffering of others all around you. Just the sound of the dog's bark can enhance the compassion that you are seeking to make the core of your life.

In this way, you can use everything that you encounter as a support for living a life based in your noble heart. You can take all your experiences as a means of growing spiritually. Nothing is intrinsically or ultimately bad. Any situation that arises is only relatively good or bad based on many factors, including—most significantly—how you perceive the situation and how you respond to it. Thus everything that appears to you can support your inner growth.

As we have seen, all of us who share this planet are closely connected. For that reason, your inner growth and the goodness you contribute to the world can truly help make the world good. You can change the world this way, from the inside out.

I had the idea once that if we each painted the corner of the world we live in with our most beautiful vision for it, those visions could be joined like pieces of a puzzle to form a vast and beautiful world. This possibility is present in every moment. We can always start by beautifying our own part of the world in whatever way we are able. Later, our picture may connect to other beautiful pictures, and in this way we can reshape the world.

Your Course through Life

The way you live your life can be your answer to the question of how you want to beautify your corner of the world. The life you live paints the world around you. As you decide where you want to go with your life, look to your interests and your capacities, as well as practical realities. If you are dedicating your life to improving your society and the world, there are no wrong choices. You can choose the issues you feel most connected to, but this does not mean you have to turn your back on other areas. It is important to remember that whatever choice you make, all the issues we have explored here are interconnected.

Whether you concern yourself with personal, social, or environmental issues, none of these are isolated from the others. We have been discussing them one by one, but they are not really separable. For instance, the issues involved in protecting the environment are very closely related to issues of food justice, and to the issues involved in social action, which in turn are linked to consumerism and greed and to conflict resolution. Maintaining healthy relationships, challenging divisions of gender, sustaining our compassion, integrating our spiritual growth into a meaningful life—these are all likewise connected. It is not as if one issue were restricted to one part of life or to a single remote corner of the world. All of us who share this planet are very much dependent on one another. Since the whole world is tightly interconnected, issues in one domain affect many others. This means that if you bring about positive change in one area, you will also have a positive effect on other areas.

No matter where you dedicate your energy, the main point is to bring your noblest aspirations to all that you do. First, create a healthy way of life consistent with those aspirations. You can start by being a good human being. Then, you can offer others around you wholesome opportunities to do the same, and actively exert yourself to bring about their happiness and well-being. In this way, your life can accomplish a twofold benefit—benefiting yourself and benefiting others.

As you ground yourself in noble aspirations, do not stop at the level of mere wishes. The aspirations that arise first within your heart are the initial links in chains of cause and effect that bring about great results in the actual world. For instance, when you are in an area suffering from complete drought, you may not be able to see anything green, even in your imagination. When it occurs to you to be the one to bring the first drop of water—to start the flow and keep it coming—a noble aspiration is born. A small but bold wish prompts you to act. From there it continues on, expanding in benefit. Your noble aspirations make you a pioneer. They make you a hero.

You may focus your efforts on one issue, but the goal is much greater. There are multiple effects you can envision, and the area you are working on at any given moment is not your only concern. Your actual goal goes far beyond that. In its broadest sense, your goal is for goodness to flow throughout the world. If you understand yourself to be acting within that vast landscape, you will always create new aspirations and gain new momentum toward fulfilling those aspirations. Your work will always be joyful.

Your capabilities may place limits on what you can accomplish at any given moment, but you can be confident that your efforts definitely affect other areas of concern far beyond those limits. Your positive impact reaches well beyond your own limitations. Whatever work you do, when you ground it in the nobility of your intentions, you help to join the whole world together in heartfelt ties of compassion.

When adverse circumstances arise, it is important not to lose your footing. If your sense of who you are is based on simply following others rather than on your own inner wisdom, then instead of standing your ground when you are challenged, you can easily be thrown off track. To stay true to yourself, it can be helpful to draw a distinction between knowledge and wisdom. Knowledge is what you learn from others. You learn by drawing on examples of other people's experience, extrapolating from what others before you have learned. Knowledge in this sense is essentially akin to imitation. Wisdom, by contrast, is discovered within yourself. Wisdom is knowledge that has surfaced from within your mind and heart.

Anchoring in Wisdom

I would like to share a story with you. During the time of the Buddha, it was customary for monks, nuns, and other religious people to beg for food each day. They subsisted on whatever food they received on their daily alms rounds.

One day, when the Buddha was out on an alms round, he arrived at the door of a well-to-do family. The owner said, "Why do you have to do this all the time, bothering us for food? You're a public nuisance. Get out! Leave us alone! You're irresponsible. Stop leeching on us. Get a real job!"

The Buddha heard him out, but didn't respond, and eventually the man ran out of steam. When the man had finished his tirade, the Buddha calmly asked him, "Are you done?"

"Yes," he said. "I'm done."

"May I ask you a question?" the Buddha said. "If someone offers you something that you do not accept, to whom does it belong?"

He said, "It would still belong to the person who was trying to give it."

The Buddha said, "Just so. And I do not accept the harsh words you have offered."

The Buddha had gained his own confidence in the truths he lived by, and so could never be deterred even slightly from following his own moral compass. But if your choices are not based in wisdom and direct self-knowledge, criticism and other external conditions can erode your confidence and sense of direction in life. On the other hand, if you have ascertained for yourself who you are and what gives meaning to your life, you can anchor yourself firmly in that wisdom. Nothing anyone says will throw you off balance. No temporary conditions will shake you up.

You need to come to know your own nature for yourself. You should know what the nature of your own mind is, and let that guide your actions. Remember that you are not a machine. Do not live the life of a robot. Be a full human being.

Lightening the Heart

The topics we have been discussing in this book are all serious. When the problems are so serious, it is not productive to add to them by being too serious ourselves. In my own life, I have faced a number of serious challenges. I have noticed from experience that taking things too seriously can be debilitating. It can paralyze us.

It is usually more effective to approach problems with a light heart—a willingness to laugh at them and at ourselves. Otherwise, if we are too somber, we could be stricken with a heart attack before we even have the chance to do anything to improve the situation! Instead, we can be playful. A sense of humor can be very helpful in preventing us from feeling stuck or overwhelmed by a difficult situation.

Especially if a situation is critical, you have to be able to approach it with some openness, just in order to see the possible solutions clearly. For example, sometimes there are serious issues that you feel you need to address, but that you cannot resolve. What do you end up doing? Worrying. There can also be serious issues that you actually can do something about. In those cases, too, if you are not careful, you may also find yourself worrying. Once you are overwhelmed by anxiety and other unhelpful emotions, it will be very difficult to plan or make clearheaded decisions. You will not be able to look beyond the obstacles to notice the opportunities.

There is a story about a Zen monk who went to collect medicinal plants. These plants were growing along the face of a steep cliff, and he had to climb down a rope to reach them. As he was climbing back up, he saw a tiger waiting for him at the top. Of course, it was a long way down if he fell, so that option looked pretty grim, too. Then, a mouse came along and started chewing on the rope. Up or down, there was no alternative but death. It was just a matter of time.

One of the medicinal plants the monk had collected had a big juicy red fruit. He took the plant out from his bag and ate the fruit right there as he clung to the rope. As the monk was chewing on it, he thought to himself, "This fruit is absolutely delicious!"

The point of this story is that the monk retained his mental freedom. Despite his dire situation, he could recognize the source of sweetness right in front of him. His response illustrates the power of keeping a wide perspective on our circumstances. He was able to keep sight of the opportunity that was right in front of him, to joyfully savor his immediate experience, even in the face of certain death.

Creating Hope Together

The challenges facing our generation and those to come are vast. But if you begin to feel weighed down by them, please remember that we will be facing them all together. None of these problems affect only one individual. They will affect us all sooner or later, in one way or another. You can take heart in the awareness that you are not the only person wanting to bring about change. When it comes to the major problems facing the world, we are truly all in this together.

On the one hand, when we look at the state of the world today, it's a pretty gloomy picture and seems to be growing darker by the day. But on the other hand, transformation and change are constant, so there is always the possibility and the hope that things can be changed for the better—if we use our intelligence and our sense of caring.

We all share the earth, and we all make our home on this planet. In this sense, we all form a single extended family. Unfortunately, much of the time we fail to see the whole picture, and only focus on the small corner we inhabit in this large home. Nevertheless, the reality is that when any two people in a family are fighting, it affects the whole family. Likewise, when two family members resolve their disputes and come together in harmony, that harmony affects the whole family. I believe it is very important to keep this wider picture in focus.

We all depend on one another. I have said this before, but I think it is worth repeating because I believe its importance cannot be overstated. We encounter endless problems when we fail to acknowledge this central fact of our interdependence. This is true on a small scale and on a large scale. If the leader of a powerful country does not have the wisdom to take into account the vast webs that bind us together, his or her decisions can have a seriously detrimental effect on people throughout the world for many years. The long-term repercussions of the systems such leaders create linger long after their incumbency, and reach far beyond what they could see with their narrow view. For example, those who helped put in place our current food systems surely did not anticipate the harmful effects we are now encountering. People in power can harm the whole country—and indeed the whole world—when they overlook the fact of our interdependence. We harm ourselves and others when we do the same.

Interdependence has many implications—practical, emotional, spiritual, and ethical. In this book, I have tried to explore some of these implications with you. Interdependence means that your happiness and mine are connected. Practically and emotionally, your happiness is bound up with the welfare of all those you are connected to or depend on. Spiritually, your happiness comes from finding the right balance of caring for others and caring for yourself. Ethically, it is right for you to respond with gratitude and kindness to those who have given you everything that you require to live and to be happy. Because you rely on others for everything you need to flourish or even just to survive, you have a responsibility to care for them. Your interdependence also means you are in a position to fulfill that responsibility, because your actions affect others deeply, too. Your awareness of interdependence is essential for the kind of positive change you want—and need—to make in the world. It is within the webs of interconnectedness that all your actions take place.

The other condition needed in order to allow you to change the world for the good is your sustained attitude of caring. Your compassionate outlook cannot merely be based on being in a supportive environment. Your loving concern for others and your commitment to act must be rooted deep within you. Live and act in the fullness of your love and affection for all beings. Take them with you wherever you go.

For the Good of the World

This meeting we have had through the pages of this book is now drawing to a close. What I have said here is not the main element in our encounter. The main element is the sincere motivation you brought to it. If you found anything helpful as you were reading, please know that the good intentions you carried with you have allowed you to hear good things, and to find useful ideas in what I have said here. It is important for you to recognize that any goodness you perceive in this book comes from your own innate goodness.

You can draw insights from your own experience. No one owns a copyright on the Buddha's teachings. They belong to the world, and in that sense they are not something I can offer to you. The teachings and teachers are ubiquitous. Reality is your teacher. Everything that appears can become your teacher. The four seasons can teach you. Anything can be a teacher of Buddhist teachings. Anything.

Now it is up to you to maintain your enthusiasm in acting for the good of the world. If you do so, anything is possible. Anything is possible, because everything arises based on the coming together of the right causes and conditions. Remember: there is no fixed starting point for you to begin from to accomplish whatever you aspire to achieve. Changing the world for the good can start from right where you are, right now. I hope you will remember this, always.

Although we may not have met in person, we need not be distant from each other mentally. Our affection for each other can keep us close. We can remain united through the goodness of our hearts. We can always see the stars twinkling in the sky. In the same way, wherever you are in the world, you can be a lamp brightening the space around you. You will always have your own light to shine. You can be a lamp dispelling not only any darkness in your own outlook, but radiating enough light to brighten the world around you as well.

In the evenings after dusk, I often go out on my terrace and look at the stars. I make the prayer now that when I do so and then close my eyes, I will be able to see you with my mind's eye, shining brightly wherever you are.

I will make prayers that many good things will come from our meeting through this book. I will pray not only for our encounter to contribute to the well-being of all beings of this world, but so that our shared prayers for goodness reach even the stars.

Our prayers and aspirations can reach far. We can see the light of stars that are thousands of light years away. Those stars may not even exist any longer, but the light they sent out can still travel and reach us here. The mind can travel even farther. There is no limit to where our aspirations can reach.

I mentioned before that we can make others the keepers of what is precious for us, when I spoke of wanting to let the moon keep my love. Since the moon is holding the love I have for you, seeing the moon can remind you of that, and inspire you. If anything I have said here makes sense to you, you can ask the moon to keep it for you. You can ask the stars to keep it for you. When you look at the moon and the stars, I hope you will be reminded of the thoughts and the love I have shared with you here.

Editors' Acknowledgments

No WORDS COULD BEGIN to acknowledge all that we received from His Holiness the Seventeenth Karmapa during our time with him in India, or in the course of preparing this book for publication. We have no hopes of repaying our debt of gratitude to him for the privilege of being part of this project.

We are grateful to many other people who made our month with the Karmapa and the production of this book possible. Our many thanks to Ngodup Tsering Burkhar, who not only offered his enthusiasm and considerable talents in interpreting for His Holiness the Karmapa, but also supported the project and students with great skill and generosity of spirit. We offer thanks as well to: Ringu Tulku, who initially proposed bringing a group of college students for extended teachings with His Holiness; Karma Chungyalpa, Deputy General Secretary of Tsurphu Labrang, for his consistent support of this project from start to finish; Khenpo Tenam and all the monks of Tsurphu Labrang, who extended hospitality and care toward us, facilitating the project in many large and small ways throughout our stay; Khenpo Lekshey, His Holiness's librarian, for creating space for us in the library in Gyuto Monastery; and Umze Bai Karma, for his time and talent in teaching the students the Tibetan chants they offered to His Holiness at the end of our stay. Our heartfelt thanks to the nuns of the Dharmadatta Nuns' Community, for graciously hosting the student group in Dharamsala.

The University of Redlands administration recognized the invitation to study with His Holiness the Karmapa as a unique opportunity in global education. Our thanks to: Professor Kelly Hankin, director of the Johnston Center for Integrated Studies, for her help in envisioning living-learning practices for our time in India, and for funding support for student travel costs; Barbara Morris, then dean of the College of Arts and Science, for her support of the course and for providing travel funds; and Sara Falkenstien, director of Study Abroad for her excellent logistical assistance.

Our deep thanks to the students in our group from the University of Redlands: Elena Cannon, Rafael Fernandes, Nina Fernando, Katie Ferrell, Jonathan Fuller, Lauren Hook, Anne Heuerman, Jakob Kukla, Brendan Mead, Brian Pines, Maya Polan, Ashley Starr, Patrick Sundolf, Jeremy Thweatt, Germaine Vogel, and Giulia Zoppolat. Thank you to Dr. Simon Barker, for joining the group and looking after our physical well-being in India. The group's commitment to the values of this project and their dedication to the hard work it entailed were conditions for its success.

We are grateful for the wise counsel of Emily Bower, our editor at Shambhala, whose guidance greatly enriched this book. Thanks, too, to our "test reader," Elizabeth Adams, for her many insightful comments.

We acknowledge with gratitude the kind sponsors of the Dharmadatta Nuns' Community, who supported Damchö throughout the year spent working on this book. We value greatly the generous ongoing support of Karen's husband, Ed Murphy, and her children, Ben and Rebekah, during Karen's monthlong absence in India, and during Damchö's visits over the course of the following year.

A Biography of His Holiness the Karmapa, Ogyen Trinley Dorje

HIS HOLINESS THE SEVENTEENTH KARMAPA was born in 1985 to a family of nomads in the remote highlands of the Tibetan plateau. He spent his formative years in one of the few remaining corners of the earth without electricity, plastics, or motor traffic. His nomadic family lived close to each other and close to the earth, shifting camp with the changing seasons in search of suitable pastures for their herds of yak and sheep. In this rugged landscape, the young Karmapa experienced a traditional Tibetan way of life that has since been virtually erased.

When the Karmapa was seven, he repeatedly demanded that his family move their camp to a certain valley, until at last they complied. Shortly after they had set up camp in the new location, several disciples of the Sixteenth Karmapa arrived in the valley. The group—a search party for the reincarnation of the Sixteenth Karmapa—had found the remote valley by following predictions and descriptions in a letter written by the Sixteenth Karmapa years before, prior to his death in 1981. Known as a prediction letter, this document comprised the Sixteenth Karmapa's instructions for locating his next reincarnation. After comparing the names of the young boy's parents and other details of his birth with the description in the Sixteenth Karmapa's prediction letter, the party declared that they had found the Seventeenth Karmapa.

From that moment onward, the Karmapa began the centuries-old course of training that would prepare him to fulfill one of the senior-most roles in Tibetan Buddhism, as spiritual leader to one of its principal orders. The school that the Karmapa heads, known as Karma Kagyu, transmits Buddhist teachings and meditation practices that were brought directly from India to Tibet a millennium ago. Since the twelfth century, the Karma Kagyu school has sought out successive reincarnations of its founder, the First Karmapa. The same system of seeking out reincarnations of major spiritual leaders was adopted throughout Tibet, including the Dalai Lama reincarnation lineage, and has contributed greatly to the continuity and resilience of Tibetan Buddhism over the centuries. Before the Karmapas pass away, they leave indications to guide their disciples through the search for their next incarnation, often in the form of letters such as the one written by the Sixteenth Karmapa.

As has been the tradition in Tibet since the seventeenth century, His Holiness the Dalai Lama was consulted and asked to confirm the recognition of the young boy as the Karmapa. His Holiness the Dalai Lama conducted his own personal investigation, and concurred that the boy was indeed the seventeenth incarnation of the Karmapa. In a rare moment in which His Holiness the Dalai Lama and the Chinese government found themselves in agreement, the Chinese authorities granted the permissions necessary in Chinese-ruled Tibet to allow the Karmapa to take his place in his monastery in central Tibet.

The Karmapa traveled from his native Kham far to the east to a nearly nine-hundred-year-old monastery in central Tibet called Tsurphu. Since its founding by the First Karmapa, each of the Karmapas has spent part of his life in Tsurphu Monastery, and it was here that the Seventeenth Karmapa was formally enthroned on September 27, 1992, with two of the three living heads of his lineage officiating. He then commenced the process of study and training that is traditional for Karmapas, yet he began offering spiritual instruction to others almost at once. At the age of eight, he delivered his first public religious discourse. The event was attended by over twenty thousand people.

In the years to come, the Karmapa would face numerous challenges in his efforts to perform his spiritual activities. His most important spiritual teachers were denied permission to enter Tibet, while the Karmapa himself failed to receive permission to travel to India to visit them. Concerned that he would be unable to perform his role as a spiritual teacher and head of a lineage, the Karmapa made a historical decision that would propel him onto the world stage. At the age of fourteen, he decided to escape from Tibet to seek freedom to fulfill his role as a world spiritual leader and to meet his responsibilities as head of the Karma Kagyu lineage.

His Holiness the Karmapa's journey began in late 1999, when he leapt from an upstairs window at night. The author himself describes the terror his group faced along the way as they fled across the Himalayas into India by jeep and on horseback, as well as on foot and by helicopter. On January 5, 2000, the Karmapa reached Dharamsala, India, where he was received personally by His Holiness the Dalai Lama. The Karmapa settled in to temporary quarters at Gyuto Monastery, a short trip from the Dharamsala residence of His Holiness the Dalai Lama, with whom he continues to enjoy a close relationship of mentor and protégé to this day.

During the twelve years the Karmapa has lived in India as a refugee, he has undergone traditional monastic training and philosophical education, while also pursuing a private modern education that includes studying science, history, English, and other languages. He has also traveled across India to participate in the cultural and religious life of his adopted home. From inaugurating temples for Sai Baba in Tamil Nadu to commemorating Mother Teresa's hundredth birthday in Calcutta, the Karmapa has met with many other spiritual leaders in a spirit of mutual respect and tolerance.

Over the years, the Karmapa has grown to play an important

role in the preservation of Tibetan culture. Tibetans have increasingly looked to the Karmapa, one of the senior-most figures in Tibetan Buddhism, for inspiration in their efforts to maintain their cultural identity in exile. He is frequently invited to speak at Tibetan schools around India, and often presides over religious ceremonies and cultural events in Dharamsala when His Holiness the Dalai Lama is traveling overseas. He paints, practices calligraphy, writes poetry, composes music, and directs theatrical events. He has written and produced several plays in Tibetan that combine elements of traditional Tibetan opera and modern theater. The performance of his first play, a drama on the life of the great Tibetan yogi Milarepa, was attended by twelve thousand people.

Along with his lessons in English and other subjects, the Karmapa's daily schedule includes time for private audiences in the mornings, and he receives tens of thousands of visitors each year from all over the world. Since 2004, he has led the annual Kagyu Monlam, a winter prayer gathering that draws thousands of attendees from different Buddhist traditions around the world. In May 2008, the Karmapa made his first trip to the West, traveling to the United States where he visited many spiritual centers under his guidance, including his North American seat in Woodstock, New York. He returned again to the States in 2011 for a second visit.

Undeterred by the challenges he has faced over the years, the Karmapa continues to transmit the spiritual teachings of his lineage, guide his students, and lead his nine-hundred-year-old school of Tibetan Buddhism into the twenty-first century.

Editors' and Translators' Biographies

Damchö Diana Finnegan
Born in New York City, Damchö Diana Finnegan worked as a journalist for seven years in New York and Hong Kong. She was ordained as a Buddhist nun in 1999 and went on to receive a PhD in Sanskrit and Tibetan Buddhist studies from the University of Wisconsin–Madison. She currently lives in Dharmadatta Nuns' Community in northern India, under the guidance of His Holiness the Karmapa.

Karen Derris
Karen Derris is an associate professor of Religious Studies and the Virginia C. Hunsaker Distinguished Teaching Chair at the University of Redlands. She earned her PhD in Buddhist Studies from the Committee on the Study of Religion at Harvard University. She lives with her husband and two children in Redlands, California.

Ngodup Tsering Burkhar
Ngodup Tsering Burkhar was born to a nomadic family near Mount Kailash in western Tibet. He escaped Tibet in 1959 and pursued his education in northern India. At a young age, he began to serve as one of the main interpreters for His Holiness the Sixteenth Karmapa. After His Holiness the Seventeenth Karmapa escaped from Tibet in 2000, Ngodup Tsering has interpreted for him as well. He is currently based in Mirik, Darjeeling, India.